I0101291

Transgenerational Gestalt Therapy

*Through the Lens of
Family Therapy in Japan*

MASATSUGU MOMOTAKE

GLASSSPIDERPUBLISHING

Edited by Vince Font

Cover design by Judith S. Design & Creativity
www.judithsdesign.com

Published by Glass Spider Publishing
www.glassspiderpublishing.com

GNJ (Gestalt Network Japan)
www.gestaltnet.jp

Contents

Acknowledgments..9

Preface 11

Chapter One: The Family Landscape 18

1.1 What is Family?..18

1.2 Feelings Are Energy 24

1.3 Family Sculpting..27

1.4 The Family Keeps on Living 31

Chapter Two: The Family's Hidden Messages..........................41

2.1 What the Family Creates 41

2.2 Feelings Resonate 43

2.3 We Assimilate Other People's Feelings...............................48

2.4 Love is a System..55

Chapter Three: What Does "Transgenerational" Mean? 63

3.1 Families Are a Refuge for the Heart 63

3.2 Transgenerational Effects 67

3.3 Anger Across Generations 73

3.4 Family Vectors 81

Chapter Four: The Theoretical Background of
Transgenerational Therapy 98

4.1 What is Gestalt Therapy? 98

4.2 Field Theory 105

4.3 The Development of Family Sculpture 116

4.4 Unresolved Problems 129

4.5 Systems of Somatic Memory 140

4.5.1 What is Somatic Memory? 140

4.5.2 The Significance of Mirror Neurons 152

Conclusion: Looking Closely at Your Ancestors 163

5.1 An Occurrence at a Street Stall 163

5.2 The Body Always Moves Toward Love 169

5.3 What Transgenerational Effects Tell Us 175

Afterword 180

About the Author 184

References 185

Acknowledgments

Transgenerational Gestalt Therapy — Through the Lens of Family Therapy in Japan was originally published in Japanese under the title *Kazoku rensa no serapi — Geshutaruto ryoho no shiten kara.* Because of its warm reception there, I thought there might be merit in sharing it with the English-speaking audience.

Owing to the hard work of Vince Font of Glass Spider Publishing, I have been able to do this. I am deeply grateful to him.

I would also like to thank Rosemary Morrison, Karen Sandness, and Atsushi Nakano of Iris International for assisting me in creating the English version.

In addition, I would like to extend my warm appreciation to Judith San Nicolas Villalonga for bringing her considerable graphic design talents to the creation of the cover.

This book was written to provide a basic introduction to Transgenerational Gestalt Therapy. The examples come from Japan, which has its own way of understanding and applying this. Though we live in the modern world, the influence of centuries of Japanese cultural patterns, ideas about the mind-body connection, and the importance of our immediate family and ancestors are evident in these examples. It may be that some of them feel foreign to the English reader. However, I hope the core principle of allowing the body to speak and aid us in our transformation toward healing will come through.

It is my sincere hope that you will all find comfort and healing in your lives.

–Masatsugu Momotake

Preface

Everyone Belongs Somewhere

My hometown is called Murakami, and it's the place where my parents are buried. If you can't quite place it, you may have heard of Senami Onsen, a hot spring resort that lies along the Japan Sea coast within the boundaries of Murakami in Niigata Prefecture. It's probably better known than the town itself. Looking for Murakami on a map, you'll find that it's on the seacoast in the northernmost part of Niigata, close to Yamagata Prefecture. It's both Japan's northernmost region, suitable for growing tea, and its southernmost region, with rivers where salmon spawn.

My mother used to go to this town every year to pay her respects at my father's grave, and I accompanied her several times. "Momotake" is a common name in Murakami, and the graves of the Momotake family are in the precincts of a temple outside of the town. We were originally more of a Shinto family, and, apparently, the family graves were on the raised paths between the rice paddies in the old days. That changed with a decree issued before World War II that stated everyone should be buried at a Buddhist temple, so we rented a corner on the grounds of this temple. My mother died a few years ago at the age of ninety-two. That's an incredibly long life, and I wonder if she lived so long because she contracted tuberculosis when she was young and learned to take good care of herself. Now my mother lies in this grave too.

Families Have Shared Primal Landscapes

Even though I call Murakami my hometown, I was actually born in a hamlet a bit inland from the town, but I'd never had occasion to visit it. One day, when my older sister came with me to visit the family graves, she told me that we had been born in a house only a twenty-minute drive from Murakami, and she took me there. What I found was nothing more than a few houses set among the rice paddies. Yet as soon as I saw this landscape, it occurred to me that it was the "other landscape" I had been seeking.

At the time I was born, my family was living in my father's parents' home in this hamlet, but a year after the end of World War II, my father took the family to Tokyo. I was still too little to walk by myself, so I encountered the hamlet as a baby carried on my mother's or grandmother's back. Even so, I found a feeling of familiarity welling up inside me.

I know this place, I thought. I wondered if this landscape of brooks and hills, seen from the point of view of a baby on an adult's back, had been imprinted on my infant memory.

My mother is from Akita, a region farther to the north, and she came to Murakami to marry my father. There she began living in this landscape. My grandparents, of course, also lived in this area, which has its own particular geography, and they saw it continuously. This suggests that the "primal landscape" of the Momotake family is one of a hamlet surrounded by rice paddies, brooks, hills, and the nearby semi-wildlands. I came to understand that my whole family shared this landscape.

Families Have Unchangeable Rules

Around the age of forty, I became interested in the world of group psychological therapy. Fortunately, Dr. Paula Bottom, a direct pupil of Fritz and Laura Perls, the creators of group therapy, was living in Japan, and I was able to study this approach with her for five years.

In these group therapy sessions, I saw situations in which people exhibited pain, anger, and dependency in their relations with their families, so it is no accident that I became concerned with families. Since people start their lives in families, I began to search for the answer to the question, "What is a family?"

During this period when I was thinking about what a family is, I encountered an extremely interesting interaction between a parent and a child. Early one summer, I had a chance to travel to the seacoast of the Izu Peninsula, and I stopped off for a cup of coffee at a restaurant that overlooked the sea. Since it was early in the morning, no other customers were there, but after a while, an older man came in with his much older mother, seemingly taking a break during their travels.

As soon as the two of them were seated, the man, who appeared to be in his sixties, began lecturing his mother, who was over eighty and had a bent back. I was sitting rather far away, but I could tell that the man was saying things like "Leave the housework up to my wife" and "Don't interfere." His wife had probably told him that she couldn't put up with his mother's behavior anymore, and he had taken her out for a drive for the specific purpose of conveying his wife's message. He was, in short, telling her to behave herself. Throughout this lecture, the bent-over old woman said nothing but just sipped her coffee.

But when the man came back from using the toilet, the older woman suddenly walked up to him and asked in a stern voice, "Did you wash your hands?" Taken aback by this unexpected reaction, he absently mumbled, "Yeah," as if acknowledging that he had, though, in fact, he had not. From that point on, the tables were turned. Thrown off-balance by his mother's unexpected show of authority, the man reverted to the parent-child interaction mode from his childhood. When the mother said, "You're a hopeless case, just a henpecked husband," this large man hunched his shoulders and listened without a word. Well, after all, she was his mother. She knew exactly the right time to go on the offense.

That scene gave me a hint about what a family might be. That is, a family has unchangeable rules. One of those rules is that relations between parents and children do not change. No matter how old the mother was, she was still the man's mother, and she would take it upon herself to tell him to "shape up."

I have learned about parent-child relations from many real-life examples. Adult sons and daughters may resist by trying to change their mothers, but something always gets in the way.

Your Body "Moves"

About that same time, I started to practice yoga by myself, and in connection with that, I began studying the Feldenkrais Method of physical training. After about ten years, I noticed something odd. One day, when I was assuming a yoga position and performing a slow Feldenkrais movement, it felt as if my body was "moving." Ever since that time, I have known that a special sensation arises in my muscles when I focus my awareness on my body. I started deliberately directing my attention to those sensations in my muscles. As I continued doing this, I realized that this feeling of movement has a certain direction, and that my body shows me what it is.

After that, these physical sensations helped me notice a more important "something" that is not taught in our current educational system—namely, that listening to my body made my life easier.

Teaching about physical sensations proved to be very useful in psychological and mental group therapy because I was able to trust what I was feeling, and this gave me an instinctive understanding of the group members' actions, words, and movements.

About Family Impasses

Experiences that families share may include difficulties or tragedies. If the family members are able to live through and overcome these shared experiences, their ties with one another will grow stronger. However, there are cases in which the family is not prepared to face difficult or tragic circumstances, or when it is not able to provide the right kind of support for its members.

Examples of difficult or tragic circumstances include witnessing the death of a family member in an accident or having a young family member develop a serious illness. In such cases, it may be difficult for the family to talk to one another. Even if individuals want to support the other members of the family, they are all facing the same problem, and they end up unable to even mention the situation.

In the field of psychological therapy, this is called an "impasse." The family members want to support one another in solving the problem, but the family as a whole suffers because no one knows how to talk about the situation. Family members share this unspoken, invisible stress in the form of physical stress. If they are unable to solve the problem, they create a family structure in which they unconsciously share the issue among themselves. This may mean that the family has chosen to continue holding on to the invisible stress.

In this book, I intend to present several examples of the ways in which a family impasse can exist within a family. I will also explain how this kind of invisible stress is passed down from generation to generation. If family members understand the systems and ways of sharing invisible stress, then they can find new pathways for moving forward

Chapter One: The Family Landscape

1.1 What is Family?

A Child with Extrasensory Perception

We have some uncanny abilities. Several years ago, I stopped off at a friend's house when a little girl from the neighborhood, who looked as if she might be in preschool or kindergarten, strolled right in and began touching the leaves of a houseplant. Without thinking, I said, "Don't touch them!" Immediately, the girl silently withdrew her hand and walked out of the house.

Yet as I watched her leave, I got the sense that she was sad. My friend's wife told me, "You know, that child can talk to plants. She likes all kinds of little creatures, and she's always talking to ants or other insects." This woman was also fond of plants and the natural world, and maybe the girl felt secure enough to reveal her innermost thoughts in her presence.

This incident reminded me of something that happened with my own daughter when she was the same age. One day around sunset, she came into the house looking happy and with her hands full of pill bugs. Immediately, her mother angrily told her, "Throw them away outside!" When I left the house the next morning, I found my daughter playing by herself in one corner of the park. She didn't notice me as I approached the spot where she was squatting and mumbling about something. There was something in the palm of her hand: the pill bugs she had thrown out the day before.

My daughter was talking to the pill bugs, and she was speaking in a tone of voice that I had never heard her use at home, a growl from deep in her throat, a voice for talking to pill bugs.

No doubt, children are born with a special ability to communicate with insects and plants. Without anyone teaching them, they talk to these other living things, touch them, and sniff them.

People can talk to plants and animals. They have the ability to not only talk to insects and other creatures, as small children do, but also to have conversations with things like rocks and mountains. I believe this is a sense humans developed during the course of their evolution as animals.

Regrettably, however, even if they once had this ability, adults in our contemporary society do not recognize the value of communication with other creatures—nor is there any kind of system for teaching children about this ability. Rather, they ignore this ability, thinking that it's meaningless or stupid. Seeing this attitude from their parents and other adults, small children give up exercising this ability to communicate with other creatures.

In this kind of society, children may either never get to develop their abilities fully or else they may take it upon themselves to abandon their own hidden abilities.

However, not all of this ability is lost. As adults, people sometimes develop a different kind of extrasensory perception. The American psychologist Abraham Maslow said something interesting. He asked university students if they had ever had any peak experiences or mysterious experiences that they'd never told anyone else about. A few students raised their hands, and he asked them to tell the other students about their experiences. Then, during the next class session, he said more students were willing to talk about their experiences.

We grow up under the influence of society, schools, and our parents' values, and these individual peak experiences and mysterious experiences are never discussed in our current educational system. We end up either ignoring them or thinking they are improbable and not talking to other people about them because we tend to believe that no one will understand them, not even our best friends or family members.

I had these kinds of experiences too, but I have to say that I felt detached from them. Rather, I thought they were foolish and didn't even take any interest in them. For that reason, when I had such experiences, I told myself, *That was amazing and mysterious.* However, I never spoke about these moments with anyone else because I believed that other people would never understand them. It may be that I didn't talk to other people about these experiences because I wanted to cherish them for myself.

One of the mysteries that we all encounter in our lives is that system known as "the family."

People do not live their lives alone. They are not born alone. They usually have a family somewhere in the background. Some people hate their families. Some people want to flee from their families. Some people have a fervent wish to stay with their families forever. However they live, people usually have a family somewhere in their background. People who think that they have not been influenced by their families have simply been ignoring this fact.

So what kind of effect do families have on people? And in what ways do people have an effect on their families?

Case 1: "Mom's Legacy of Symptoms"

Several years ago, a woman came to me complaining of headaches. The pain was not particularly severe, nor did they incapacitate her, but she described them in words such as "My head always feels heavy" and "I have a throbbing pain in my head."

As we talked about this pain, she suddenly realized something. Her mother had had headaches. In fact, she had been plagued by them.

"Now that you mention it, " she said, "from the time I was a little girl, I can't tell you how often I had to listen to my mother say that she had a headache."

When she told me that, I noticed that her eyes were shining with a sort of nostalgia. She bowed her head slightly and seemed to be experiencing the feeling, even holding a silent conversation with someone.

"I started having headaches at the same age that my mother did."

"My mother died several years ago."

"I am the same age that my mother was when she died."

"Developing headaches was a way of remembering my mother."

She said, "When I got to be the same age as my mother, I started to understand her." The woman was now raising a daughter of her own, and this awoke in her memories of her own childhood. As she saw her daughter playing up to her to get her own way, complaining, enjoying her food, and crying angry tears, she felt,

"My mother took care of me in this same way."

There were times when feelings of gratitude toward her mother welled up inside her, but within the busy daily routines of childcare, these feelings lasted only a moment. In the next moment, she was pulled back into the realities of taking care of her daughter. She had no time to immerse herself in memories of her mother, which evaporated amid the preoccupations of everyday life.

"What if these headaches are a way to summon my mother's presence while I'm involved in taking care of my daughter?"

Now it makes her happy to imagine her mother's voice saying, "I have a headache," just as she did throughout her childhood.

This woman was expressing her memories of her mother in the form of a physical symptom. The pain in her head brought forth a sense of security, a feeling that she was with her mother. Oddly enough, once the woman realized this, her headaches vanished, but she now felt that her mother would always be inside her.

People have uncanny abilities. Sometimes, they even use their own bodies to assure themselves of the existence of their families.

1.2 Feelings Are Energy

The following example should be familiar to many readers, even though it doesn't involve any physical symptoms.

Case 2: "I Sound Just Like My Mother"

One client told me that she was shocked to realize she sounded exactly like her mother when she scolded her children. From early childhood, she had always told herself that she would never become the kind of emotional woman her mother was. That's why she was so surprised to hear herself yelling at her children in exactly the same way her mother had yelled at her.

My client's mother was short-tempered and always yelling at her and her older brother. Sometimes, she even threw a teacup at them if she happened to be holding one. Like a typical teenage boy, her brother just gruffly told their mother to "shut up and leave [him] alone."

However, my client was afraid of her mother's bursts of temper. When her mother was in a bad mood, she even took it out on her husband. She used to screech at him and browbeat him in front of the children.

Having grown up in this kind of household, this client promised herself, "I never, ever want to turn out like my mother." She made such an effort to be unlike her mother that during her elementary and middle school years, her friends described her as "sweet."

Yet once she married and had children, she began to feel anger welling up within her. She flew into rages over even the most trivial problems. She felt that she was gradually turning into a bad-tempered person like her mother, and she hated herself for it. What could she do about this?

That was when I explained to her that **she acted this way because it had some sort of meaning for her**. We try to change our actions when we don't like the way we're acting. However, when we look at this phenomenon in psychological terms, continuing to act in an undesirable way **means something to us**, so taken together, these attitudes and actions make up our behavior.

In that sense, we keep repeating the same actions, unless we happen to take notice of them. Our rational mind may regret our actions, but even if we think, "I have to stop letting my emotions get the better of me" or "This attitude can't possibly be good for my children," we find anger welling up within us.

I told my client what she should do the moment she realized that she was yelling at her children. I recommended she should ask herself what she was trying to express. Of course, I also advised her not to blame herself or feel regret when she was angry, and to not try to suppress her anger. The purpose was **to**

make her feel what was happening in her body when she was angry at her children, because the moments in which she was truly angry were the moments in which she understood what she was doing.

Inheriting Her Mother's Energy

When I met this client two weeks later, she looked calm and relaxed, so I was eager to find out what she had noticed. As she spoke, I learned that at first, the old pattern of blaming herself emerged when she scolded her children, and she recalled how she had hated her mother's emotional outbursts.

However, during the second week, she noticed a feeling of pleasure coursing through her as she yelled at her children. "That's not what I expected!" she told herself, but sure enough, she felt a comfortable, pleasurable feeling throughout her body.

From then on, she began to feel that there was some sort of meaning to her anger, and she finally realized it had to do with her role as the mother of the family. Her mother had operated a business, and she was naturally busy running this family business. The business was not large enough to need employees, so it was entirely dependent on her mother's abilities.

As the oldest daughter, her mother inherited the business instead of her brothers, who were unreliable. Having been a child at the time, my client had no idea how this had happened, but evidently, everyone had acknowledged her mother as the head of the family and someone who had a talent for managing a business.

My client realized that she, too, wanted to work as her mother had. She found herself thinking, "I'm like my mother in having an excess of energy and talent." She began to sense that she, like her mother, would find work that allowed her to express herself fully.

In an unexpected turn of events, she stopped thinking of her two children as annoying. Instead, she began to see them as little balls of energy. "They have inherited my energy," she concluded. "Of course they have, because they're my children, and they have inherited my characteristics, just as I inherited my mother's powerful energy." She said that this realization only intensified her love for her children.

1.3 Family Sculpting

One experience in particular motivated me to start thinking about the topic of families. It took place fifteen or more years ago, during the era when phrases like "voluntary shut-in" and "refusal to attend school" were gaining currency in Japan.

Around that time, Professor Hiroshi Inamura of Tsukuba University (former Professor of Medicine at Hitotsubashi University, 1935-1996) was conducting family therapy for parents whose children refused to go to school, a phenomenon that was already being called "school refusal." I was also interested in this problem and invited Professor Inamura to attend one of my sessions.

Case 3: The Father Who Didn't See His Family

A man came to me complaining, "I'm at a loss for what to do because my children are refusing to go to school."

The approach Professor Inamura used impressed me. He asked the man about the people who comprised his family, and then he chose people among the participants to appear in front of the group and portray the members of the man's family.

He had these people stand, and, after asking the man which direction each member should be facing and how far apart they should be, he arranged them accordingly. Once he did that, the distribution of the family members showed us a surprisingly accurate picture of the truth about the family.

The mother and the elementary-school-age daughter were standing facing each other with little distance between them. The middle-school-age son was also standing fairly close to his mother and looking at her. He was also standing next to his sister, which we could interpret as meaning that he got along well with her.

However, the man portraying the father was located outside the space that the rest of the family was occupying and facing in a direction unrelated to any of the others. It was obvious at a glance that the father was not part of the family circle.

This simple method was an approach that yielded extremely interesting results. The group understood the structure of the family immediately.

The person portraying the father stood rooted with his back to his family, his attention directed toward his job.

Professor Inamura then asked the participants portraying the family members how they felt about the distances between them and the directions in which they were facing.

The woman playing the mother replied, "It felt very comfortable and pleasant." The person who portrayed the daughter replied, "I was so close to my mother that I felt smothered." The person who portrayed the son replied, "I felt secure having my mother and sister nearby, but in the end, I sensed that I am being controlled by my mother." Finally, the man who portrayed my client replied, "My interest is focused on my work, and I am not aware of my family."

By seeing the distances and the directions adopted by the people who portrayed the family members, anybody could see what was happening in my client's family. In fact, it may be more accurate to say that rather than understanding the true nature of the family, we were able to **see** it.

Everyone sensed that the daughter refused to go to school. Furthermore, everyone could **see** beyond all doubt that the father was enthusiastic about his work but had turned his back on his family.

My client, the actual father of the family, **saw** the true state of his family. A week later, we held another group session in which my client spoke haltingly about how he had tried to establish communication with his family by taking them all to a karaoke club. Seeing the true shape of his family had prompted him to take a small first step.

Professor Inamura called this approach "family sculpture." This first experience of seeing relationships within the family in three-dimensional terms, including distance and direction, is indelibly engraved on my mind.

There is another reason that the "Family Sculpting" approach impressed me so deeply: it does exactly the same thing as Gestalt therapy. In Gestalt therapy, we use what we call the "empty chair" approach.

In this dialogue-based method, we try to figure out the human and dynamic relationships among family members by placing chairs or cushions representing the father or mother in the room. We then have the client speak to the chairs or cushions as if their father or mother were actually there.

This approach makes the relationship between parents and children, and the complex relationships among family members, **visible in a way that outsiders can see**. Through this process, clients gain a deeper insight into themselves.

1.4 The Family Keeps on Living

Case 4: A Dialogue with a Dead Child

At times, I have been forced to think further about family bonds. One such occasion was when I was invited to a regional city to attend a support group for women who had experienced a miscarriage or stillbirth. I heard about their profound experiences with these tragedies.

One woman had suffered several miscarriages. She now had living children and felt happy and content, but even so, she said, "My heart aches when I think about my stillborn child. I reminisce and think, 'If only that baby had lived.'" Another woman said that she was tormented by her own a sense of responsibility for the loss of the child. "I feel so sorry for this baby," she said sadly. "It's my fault that it never had a chance to live in this world."

Another woman, who'd suffered a miscarriage due to her husband's abuse, had had secret troubling thoughts over a period of twenty years: "The fact that I was pregnant with that baby couldn't even protect me."

One by one, the women spoke to one another as women, mothers, and parents about their deep love for their child. As I listened to each woman telling her experience and the thoughts hidden deep in her heart, sharing her sorrow and pain with the other members of the group, a miracle occurred.

The first woman who told her story suddenly gave a little cry. "Oh, that baby was a boy!" The look in her eyes made it obvious that she could see the baby clearly. I told her to speak to the boy.

After doing so, she turned to me with a joyful look on her face. "He smiled at me when I talked to him."

Another woman had a conversation with her child, who had been stillborn four years previously. As the conversation was coming to an end, she gasped in a combination of astonishment and relief. "Oh, my, she's grown into a four-year-old girl." Oddly enough, whenever she thought of that baby, it was always in terms of "if she were still alive . . ." and here she was, appearing to her mother in the form of a four-year-old.

Still another woman reported that her child smiled and assured her, "I'm fine." One child smiled and said, "Goodbye." Another child told his mother, "Look how much I've grown."

The session in which these various dialogues occurred was not very long, but I found it to be very moving because as the mothers spoke with their children, those children grew into the age they would have been if they had lived.

Mothers have the ability to sense this, the ability to see their children. It is one of the most uncanny abilities human beings sometimes manifest, abilities that may be due to the power of family ties. Children who are born into a family continue to live within that family whether they are alive or dead.

By "continuing to live," I don't mean only that babies who are miscarried or stillborn live on in the hearts of their family members. This concept includes adults who have left home or who have cut off all ties with their relatives. Spouses who get divorced due to finding themselves unable to live together are also included in this definition of "continuing to live."

What I am trying to say is that "continuing to live" means more than memories or recollections of past experiences. **What I mean is that they are literally living with their families here and now.**

Puzzling Out Unresolved Emotions

In recent years, the younger generations in Japan have come to lose their resistance to the word "counseling." However, instead of going for counseling or therapy to seek solutions for the psychological problems plaguing them, a steadily increasing number of them are going to counseling to get hints about how to design their future or about what paths their lives should follow.

A situation that came up when I was teaching one unit of a corporate training course may be a sign of the times. I was explaining that **individuals' unresolved emotions lie behind interpersonal problems in the workplace**.

I asked the participants to think of a supervisor or boss or anyone else who ranked above them in their individual workplaces that they couldn't get along with. Then I had them imagine a situation in which that supervisor or boss was moving toward them. After that, I had them envision a supervisor or boss they liked moving toward them. Finally, I asked them what physical reactions they had in each situation.

Case 5: Seeking the Absent Father

During this exercise, a woman in her early thirties expressed her opinion. She was seeking to establish herself in a career, and so far, everything in her work life and private life was proceeding according to plan. Her own efforts appeared to have earned her the life she wanted. There was just one exception . . .

The exercise we had just conducted had made her realize that she was conflating both the supervisor she couldn't get along with and the supervisor she liked with her mother.

"I think I'm projecting both my anger and my respect for my mother on those two supervisors. I treat the supervisor I don't get along with as representing the unacceptable aspects of my mother, and I superimpose the aspects that I recognize as her more human characteristics on the supervisor that I like. And when I realized that I was conflating the things I hated and respected about my mother with those two supervisors, a change occurred in my body.

"What kind of change? Well, when I feel angry at my mother, I feel a surge of strength on the right side of my body. I clench my right fist, and my right shoulder stiffens," she laughed. "So I guess I'm really angry.

"And what's really strange is that I feel that all pain is disappearing from the left side of my body. Actually, I have several kinds of pain on my left side, my left wrist, left shoulder, and left knee. I used to think that I was injuring that side somehow. The moment I thought about the supervisor I liked, I could feel warm blood flowing into my left side. I wonder what my left side was reacting to. I'd be interested to find out."

In answer to her question, I asked, "How many people are there in your family?"

"There are four of us," she replied, "my younger brother, my mother, my grandmother, and myself. My mother and grandmother still live in the house where I grew up, but my brother is married and has his own home."

Since she was constantly at odds with her mother, she had gone to a university in Tokyo and lived there ever since. Now she hardly ever returned to her family home because seeing her mother was emotionally distressing.

When I asked about her father, she said, "He left us when I was a baby, and my parents got divorced. I've never met him."

I decided to have her tell me a little more about her mother. According to her, it seemed her mother had struggled through life as a single mother. For whatever reason, she had never given her daughter a chance to see her father. The woman had grown up without a father, and her mother, being a strong woman, had performed the roles of both parents. For that reason, the woman had only a vague notion of her father.

For all expressed purposes, the woman explained, "I don't have a father."

Despite that answer, I couldn't help noticing that she kept

stroking her left elbow. She noticed me staring and became aware of her own words about how she had pain only on her left side.

She asked, "What does it mean that my pain is only on my left side?" Even though she was asking me, she also seemed to be asking herself the same question. "No, that can't be it, but . . ."

Awareness Arises Out of Feeling

She seemed to be sensing something, a sensation that she couldn't put into words, even though she knew that it was meaningful. She was experiencing something, but it felt as if she was hesitant to say anything about it.

Finally, she declared, "My father is on my left side!" She was looking at a space about three meters away to her left.

Even though she was a bit confused about it, she sensed the presence of her father in the spot she was looking at. At the same time, she suddenly realized that the sadness, unease, coldness, and irritation she thought were feelings about her mother were actually her feelings about her father.

Ever since she was a small child, she had been seeking her father. When she visited the homes of friends whose fathers lived with them, she thought she would be so happy if her father could be with her, too. However, she had never asked her mother about him because, even as a small child, she somehow realized from her mother's attitude that such questions were unwelcome. Even so, she had never lost her love and longing for her father. In addition, she'd not only never asked about her father directly but had decided not to even mention him. At the same time, her body had found an unconscious means of feeling love for her father.

In the world of psychological therapy, we call these kinds of phenomena "awareness" or "insight." This means that as we dig deeper into people's psychological processes, the answers they seek come welling up from within them.

Some people even literally hear these answers as spoken words. Sometimes, people like the woman in this example suddenly generate an image. Unlike auditory or visual hallucinations, however, these sounds and sights **have a therapeutic effect on the client**. They're like the final piece of a puzzle fitting exactly into the last remaining blank space.

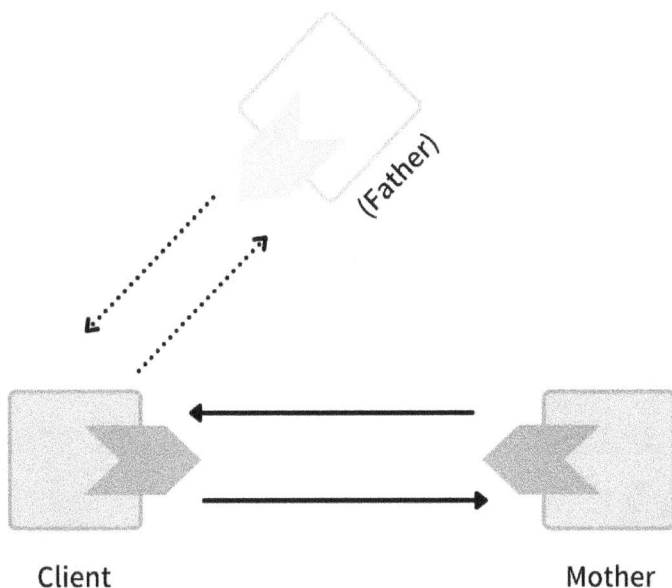

Client   Mother

The client has been made aware of her interactions with her mother.

The client's father has remained alive near her, to her left, and she has quietly accepted this fact. I really look forward to seeing what kinds of changes will occur in her body and health as a result.

Furthermore, I want to find out the effects of this awareness on her relations with the opposite sex and sense of values with respect to her family.

I do not know of any scientific explanation for these kinds of physical effects. However, people's bodies are equipped with uncanny antennae, and with these antennae, they receive messages about their families.

Chapter Two: The Family's Hidden Messages

2.1 What the Family Creates

There Are No Good or Bad Emotions

We all have two sets of emotions. The first set consists of our individual emotions, which let us feel that something is fun or that we are sad. We meet someone, and we think, "I'm glad I met you" or "I'd like to see you again." These are stirrings of the heart that arise from individual experiences.

The second set consists of emotions that arise from family systems. Families have words and values that are used only within the group. They may be family secrets that outsiders don't know about or may be based on experiences that only members of the family have shared.

So what significance do emotions have for human beings? Even within the fields of psychology and mental health therapy, there are many viewpoints about emotions and ways of understanding them. Some specific schools of thought and theories analyze emotions and try to assign meanings to them. Other schools of thought think of emotions as things that ought to be controlled.

However, the point of view I prefer is that our emotions are meaningful, not when they are controlled but when they are expressed, because there is no such thing as a good emotion or a bad emotion. We acquired emotions in the process of our evolution just as birds acquired wings, lions acquired fangs, spiders acquired the ability to spin webs, and horses acquired agile legs. Even though carnivores have fangs, they aren't evil. Porpoises live in the ocean, catch fish, and have the ability to jump, but it is meaningless to judge these traits as good or evil. For humans, the process of evolution chose to have humans develop emotions as the best way for their lineage to continue.

Emotions Express the Self as It Is, Here and Now

In therapeutic practice, therefore, even if you hate someone so badly that you'd like to kill them, we don't label that as a "negative emotion" or anything like that. We make sure not to label emotions as "positive" or "negative" because those feelings give us a hint of your relations with that person.

Emotions exist to help us understand our own experiences. For example, if you are on a commuter train or some other crowded place and someone steps on your foot, your initial reaction might be surprise or anger or even rage, and you may want to demand that the other person apologize. Nobody whose foot has been stepped on is going to say, "Thanks" or "I'm so glad" or otherwise be full of gratitude. Emotions exist to tell us what kinds of experience we are having **here** and **now**, so the emotions we need are generated inside of us when the situation demands it.

Feelings of anger arise when someone attacks or insults us or makes a caustic remark. This kind of anger is "attack energy." When someone tries to hurt or attack us, we use that energy to protect ourselves by attacking the person in return. We are animals, and animals have teeth to protect themselves, teeth they acquired to chew the meat and plants that are their food.

Feelings of joy come from happy experiences. When we happen upon landscapes that delight us, joy and excitement well up within us. We are happy when we have a lively conversation with friends or when we're watching our favorite sport. On the other hand, when we experience sorrow or loneliness, sad feelings well up within us. Emotions are important sensations that human beings acquired in the course of evolution. They tell us the meaning of what we are experiencing at any time and in any place.

2.2 Feelings Resonate

In this sense, an individual's feelings operate according to extremely simple principles. However, the second type of feelings don't really belong to you. Instead, they arise from your family system and from relations among the people who make up your family. Yet since the sources of those feelings have been an integral part of your family since the time you were born, you believe that they are your own feelings. In fact, they are feelings that arose from your relations with your family, but you end up thinking that the tensions that arise among your relatives are solely your problem.

Case 6: "My Two Selves Are Beating Up on Me"

The other day, I had a chance to speak with a woman in her thirties who already owned two fashion shops. During the course of our conversation, she said, "I'm always beating up on myself."

"Why do you say that?" I asked, not having expected that remark. Having managed to acquire two shops at such a young age, she struck me as being a bit stuck-up and curt. She spoke confidently and rapidly, giving the impression of having an assertive personality. However, you don't really understand someone else's feelings unless you talk with them.

This woman had worked hard, much harder than most people, to acquire her shops. Even so, there seemed to be two "selves" inside her, each one constantly criticizing the other. One "self" was the ambitious personality, putting all she had into her work. But then her other self would start to scold her with complaints like, "Can't you take it easy?" or "You're always such a work horse," or "Don't you ever settle down?" or "I'm all worn out." In fact, she had overworked to the point of collapsing from exhaustion.

However, when she listened to the "self" that wanted to rest, the other "self" would start to nag her, saying, "Is that all you can do?" or "You sure are lazy," or "You can't go on living alone." Relaxing was almost painful, so she would throw herself into her work again.

After hearing what she said, I asked, "Aren't both of those 'selves' actually you? Each one criticizes and beats up on the other." That's when I gave her some analogies to think about.

Animals and plants never scold themselves, and I don't think that such a living creature exists. Ants don't say things like, "Why am I a worker ant? I'm too busy." The butterflies in the sky certainly don't think, "Why did I have to be a caterpillar before I could become a butterfly?" Other living creatures just enjoy their lives as best they can. Since they enjoy their lives, they produce descendants. They live in the moment and taste its joys fully, and that's why they want to increase their kind. Humans are the same. Before we are humans, we are living creatures. We are animals. We were not born to beat up on ourselves. If our hominid ancestors had been like that, humans would never have left any descendants.

I told her that she must have somehow learned to scold herself.

A few days after our conversation, she came back to continue where we had left off. "Actually," she explained, "the two selves are my father and mother." After she returned home, a number of memories came to mind. Her father had always criticized her mother with words like, "You're a complete mess," or "You never do anything." Meanwhile, her mother had complained about her father in terms such as, "You're always so grumpy about your work," or "I wish you'd help around the house just a little."

When she remembered these scenes, a memory of a quarrel between her parents came to mind. "When I was in elementary school," she recalled, "I always sat with my back to my parents as they rehashed the same old arguments, and I avidly watched music shows on TV. No, it may be more accurate to say that I kept my eyes glued to the TV. That's how I was when I was a child. I focused in on the TV so that I couldn't sense or hear my parents fighting behind me.

"I became extremely nervous. I was always terrified at those times. But even so, I didn't turn around and look at them. I didn't do anything except stare at a TV show. The real me was anxious, a little elementary-school kid who felt that she didn't belong anywhere.

"Even after I grew up, I was full of anxiety. I noticed that this anxious person was my real self, and when that feeling came over me, I realized that the self that wanted to take it easy had absorbed my mother's personality, while the self that worked hard had absorbed my father's vitality. My parents got divorced when I was a child, and my father drifted away from us, so I didn't see him. Still, I realized that I loved both my mother and my father.

"Ever since I was a child, I wanted to bring the two of them together. When I thought of my mother, I recalled my father's voice, and when I thought of my father, I recalled my mother's voice.

"I finally understood that my anxiety was not my problem but something that had grown out of the friction between my parents. I had incorporated the conflict between my parents into myself, and now, as an adult, I understand that it's not my responsibility. That's why I decided to send my anxiety back to my father and to my mother."

The woman explained that she is glad she inherited her father's social vitality and feels pride in her own success. At the same time, she is now able, like her mother, to accept the need to relax at home when she is tired.

Children absorb their parents' values and views about life, which become guidelines for their own lives. Sometimes, they reject their parents' values and views about life, and even though they believe they are creating their own new values, they take their parents as examples of what not to do. Such people may react to their upbringing and assume attitudes that are the direct opposite of what they were taught, but these are not their own values. It's just that their standards are 180° from those of their parents.

If a family enjoys success in society, the values of the parents or grandparents who made the family's success possible often become that family's rule of life. If the ancestor was an entrepreneur, the family's basic values may focus on the size of the company or the scale of the operation. Families that enjoy name recognition in society or have a record of academic achievements may evaluate family members on the basis of their educational records or social success. Family members who meet these standards receive positive recognition from the family, but members who do not meet these standards may end up being less valued.

2.3 We Assimilate Other People's Feelings

Let's return to the subject of our two types of feelings. We have feelings that arise from our experiences here and now: stirrings of the heart and emotions based in our current circumstances. We can control them in some ways. If we want to experience certain feelings of enjoyment or excitement again, we meet up with a friend, go on a trip, or find some kind of work that we like. In other words, we decide what we want to do and make it happen. We can even accept sorrow and anger, as when we are sad after breaking up with someone we love, or if we're angry at our boss. Even so, we cannot really control our feelings, only the circumstances that motivate them.

However, we really can't control the second type of feelings. These are more difficult because they do not arise out of anything that we are responsible for. No matter how much we want to regulate our moods, it's hard to do so because they do not arise out of our experiences. The feelings that arise out of family systems sometimes make us feel powerless. Since these feelings are accompanied by a sense that we can't change them just because we want to, we end up being demoralized by them.

These emotions of the second type are often experienced as if they are our own feelings. For that reason, unless we become aware that they arise from our family systems, they do not go away. I'd like to present a couple of case histories that illustrate this point.

Case 7: "I Feel My Partner's Stress in My Body"

A woman named Michiyo Abe told me about the following situation.

"I feel as if I'm not accepted by my family. There are three of us: me, my husband, and our daughter. It's not that relations among us are bad, but I still feel uncomfortably ill at ease. I don't feel that way at work, just when I'm at home. It's the feeling that my family doesn't really accept me as I am. It all makes me anxious, and I want to know where that anxiety comes from."

She felt this anxiety as a lump of tension in her lower abdomen, and she wondered what that tension was and what it meant. Up until that point, she had been unaware of the connection between her feelings and her body.

That was when I decided to have her recreate the experience of having uncomfortable feelings concentrated in her lower abdomen. I wanted to have her experience the feeling of not being accepted by her family, and to discern the meaning of that feeling, I decided to look at her "family sculpture."

I had her illustrate the relations among the three members of the family by placing them in positions that demonstrated those connections.

I asked her to express the relations between herself, her husband, and their daughter in terms of distance.

Then, to clarify the relations among the three of them further, I asked her to designate the direction in which they were facing so that I could gain an overall picture of the situation. The family sculpture that she ended up with was as follows:

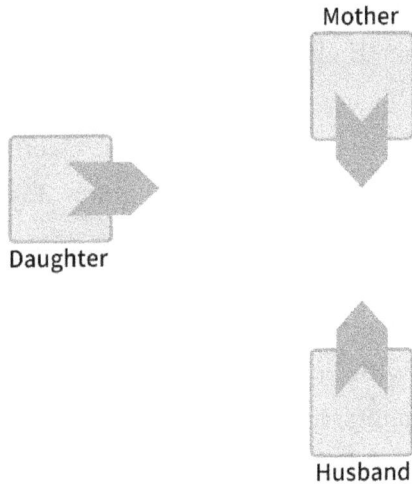

Mother

Daughter

Husband

We can see that she is closer to her husband than to her daughter. Usually, mothers place their daughters closer than their husbands. If that's the case, what is the meaning of Michiyo's feeling ill at ease?

Could it be her close relationship with her husband, or is it connected to her having a more distant relationship with her daughter than with her husband? Is her feeling of not being accepted due to her relationship with her husband or her relationship with her daughter?

A short distance between people often means their relationship is close. Thinking in those terms, Michiyo may be having more problems with her relationship with her daughter than with her husband.

Next, we look at the direction everyone is facing. Both her husband and her daughter are facing her. I believe this is consistent with Michiyo's statement that "it's not that relations among us are bad," because if the husband were facing in some other direction and facing the daughter, that might mean something else.

I told Michiyo to have a talk with her daughter; to have her start a conversation with her. The ideas that came through in the course of the conversation included "I want to have my mother take care of me more" and "I want to be with her." The daughter unconsciously revealed her loneliness as she said things like, "I do like kindergarten, but I wish you'd hug me more." It seemed that Michiyo had expressed her distant relationship with her daughter in terms of physical distance. It represented the way in which her daughter was putting up with the loneliness that came from wanting to depend more on her mother and wanting to be hugged.

Next, we looked at Michiyo's relationship with her husband. At that point, she complained that a knot of tension was developing in her lower abdomen. That was the source of feeling ill at ease at home.

"You never tell me anything, and that makes me anxious!"

These words were directed at her husband. However, her husband was apparently a kind man and never complained to her. He never said anything like "This is what I'd like you to do in your role as my wife" or "This is what I'd like you to do in your role as a mother" or "This is what I'd like you to do for our daughter."

His favorite expressions were "That's fine" and "Do whatever you like." He was in no way dismissive of her. Instead, it felt as if whatever his wife wanted really was fine with him. Yet Michiyo suddenly understood that these interactions made her anxious. Her husband's failure to say clearly, "I don't like that" or "I'd like you to do this" made her nervous.

It seemed, then, that the source of her anxiety was her husband's habit of never expressing an opinion or indicating his true feelings or stating what he wanted. This was what made her feel ill at ease.

Oddly enough, when she placed herself in his position, her stressful feelings intensified. It was as if her husband had that same knot of tension in his lower abdomen, and she had copied it. We often see this kind of phenomenon in psychological therapy. One person's stress is felt by the other family members, each of whom perceives it as "my stress."

If her feelings of uneasiness came from her husband's stress, then she would not be able to rid herself of that anxiety, because it was not *her* anxiety or *her* uneasiness. So why did this kind of thing happen? Why did Michiyo feel her family's anxiety?

Many people are plagued by anxiety, anger, sadness, or guilt that they think of as their own emotions. In fact, these are often feelings they have absorbed from members of their family, the result of emotional resonance with the people they love.

Michiyo's husband lost his father due to illness when he was just a child. Apparently, this loss made him feel anxious about his role as a father. Even when he felt annoyed or dissatisfied with his wife or daughter, he suppressed those feelings and never expressed them. Instead, they manifested themselves as a knot of tension in his abdomen. Michiyo was reacting to that tension with sensitivity, and it may be fair to say that she had assimilated her husband's emotions.

When people become aware of the meanings of the sensations and emotions they feel, they experience the relief of having those feelings disappear, because the message their body is trying to send has been received. The longer people — whether in families, workplaces, or other groups — share time and space, the stronger the ties among them become. In such an environment, the members of the group absorb the feelings that others are not expressing. In other words, their emotions resonate.

If families and specific groups are together for a long time, a special "venue" comes into being. This invisible venue is where group members exchange invisible messages with one another.

2.4 Love is a System

Case 8: The Son Who Wanted to Kill His Father

A young man who I'll call "Kawanaka" was in his twenties when he came to me worried about wanting to kill his father.

"I don't know why I feel that way," he said. Then he added a statement that contradicted the first: "I know why I want to kill my father." However, what really worried him was that he couldn't suppress that emotional impulse.

Something didn't quite add up, so I decided to listen to his story. According to him, all his father did was make demands on his mother, and Kawanaka found that unacceptable. When I asked him for an example of one of those demands, he said, "My father borrowed some money, and my mother assumed responsibility for it and paid it back."

He also gave me several other instances. "For example, Dad can't get started on something without consulting Mom, even if it's something that he wants to do. And even when Mom is sick, he never helps her in the kitchen. He's quit his job several times. He's always playing up to Mom to get her to do things for him."

I asked him, "Have you ever had an argument with your father that made you want to kill him?"

Kawanaka's answer made even less sense. "No," he said. "My father is already dead, so that has never happened."

I took a deep breath and tried to confirm his statement. "You mean that you're upset because, even though you want to kill your father, you can't do it because he's dead?"

His answer was similar to the previous one. "No, the reasons I want to kill my father are easy to understand, but even I know that there's nothing I can do about it. What bothers me is that even though I don't want my mother to suffer, my father is dependent on my mother."

I was exasperated with him and asked, "But if your father is dead, he can't make her suffer anymore, can he?"

He replied: "No, but I can't forgive my father for doing that."

At this point, I realized that Kawanaka was in conflict with the father who survived in his mind. He felt as if his father was still alive. That's when I decided to have him create a family sculpture.

"Please try arranging the members of your family in this space," I said.

His family consisted of four people: his parents, himself, and his younger sister. I had him represent the relationships between them in terms of distance and direction. For some reason, this young man did not include his sister in the family space. That was also meaningful, but I decided to have him proceed with just his parents and himself.

First, I had him place himself in the center and decide the distance between himself and his parents. Next, I had him decide which direction each of the three people was facing.

The resulting arrangement formed a triangle, with each person placed about one meter away from the other two. I saw that both the young man and his father were facing the mother, and I realized that the energy of both the father and the son was directed toward the mother.

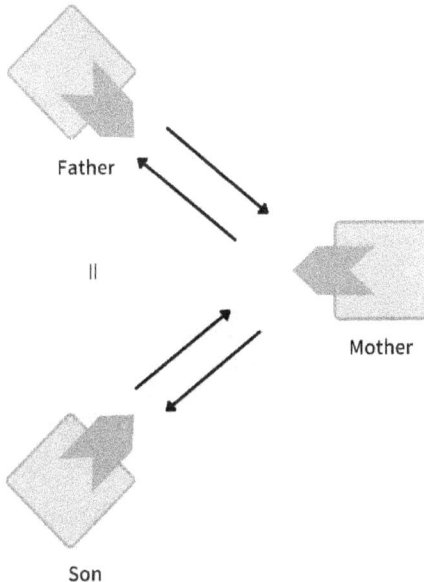

Father

||

Mother

Son

It should be obvious from the drawing that the energy in this family was focused on the mother, and the direction in which this energy was flowing had a special meaning. The father was drawn in by the mother's kindness, and it was easy to see that he depended on her. Yet it was interesting to see that Kawanaka's energy was also directed toward his mother. He, too, seemed to be drawn in by her loving nature.

One could interpret this diagram as meaning that father and son were rivals for the mother's love, and it's possible to observe all sorts of things based on distance and direction in this kind of family structure. As the Japanese version of the famous proverb puts it, "Hearing a hundred times is not equal to seeing once." The family sculpture provided a lot of visual information and brought to light much more than what Kawanaka had told me.

I instructed him to move around to each position in turn and then sit down. I had him tell me what kind of posture his mother assumed when she was facing her husband and son, and what she was saying.

Then I asked him to move to the father's position, sit down in the posture that his father would have assumed, and think about how his father would have felt. I instructed him to feel what the words spoken in such a posture would represent to his mother. Then I asked Kawanaka to explain in his own words how he would talk to his mother from each position in the family sculpture.

I had him add posture as the third element in this sculpture, after **distance** and **direction**. Adding the respective **postures** created a three-dimensional world.

These interactions made it clear that Kawanaka was trying to assume his father's role. In other words, he acted more like a husband than a son when dealing with his mother. For that reason, the direction he faced when he was in his father's position was the same direction he faced when he was in his own position.

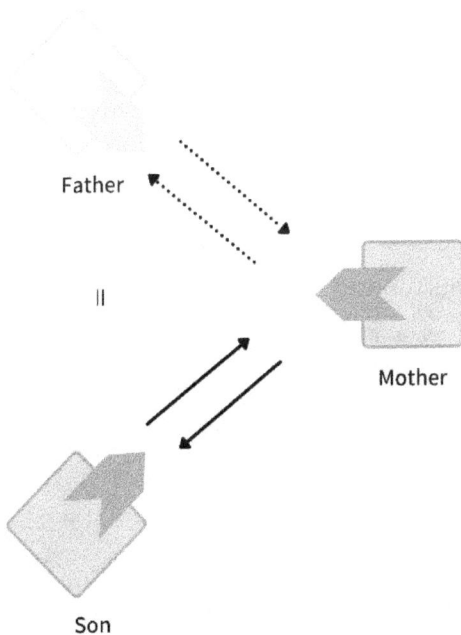

Undertaking a Role That Was Missing in the Family

When a family is missing one of its members, someone else takes over that role. If a family has lost its mother, the oldest daughter, even if she is still a child, sometimes begins to do the cooking, laundry, and shopping to take care of the rest of the family. Similarly, Kawanaka wanted to help his mother, so he unconsciously assumed the father's position and began acting like him. Sons who have lost their fathers sometimes enter the workforce early and try to support their family economically, and sometimes the family even asks them to do that.

In this case, however, Kawanaka had done something else. He had stopped attending school. People sometimes choose odd methods to attain their objectives. They act on the basis of unique values that pertain only within the fixed family structure, and Kawanaka chose to stay home from school, which would allow him to remain at his mother's side all the time. It may have been a sign of his love for his mother. At the same time, he could take over the portion of love that his father had felt for his mother, even as he caused her endless problems. I began to feel a vague sense of the meaning of Kawanaka's omission of his sister from the family sculpture space. Here is where the family's invisible, unspoken rules came into play.

There is no clear answer to the question of why the members of this family express their love in this way. However, families have invisible rules; values that operate within the family but are hidden from outsiders; values that have been silently cultivated within the family over time.

The hidden message in this family may have been "The most important thing in life is being loved by Mother." On the other hand, it may have been "Mother's love for the family is the most important value in life." These kinds of rules are probably more important to a family than society's rules. The hidden message may be "You are helpless, so I will rescue you" or "You're no good without me." In this case, the "I" is the mother, but in some cases, the father and the son may be the "I."

Another conceivable possibility concerns the father's absence. In such cases, the dynamic in which the son takes over the father's role is intensified, and he responds to the family's hidden demands, perhaps by dropping out of college for economic reasons and getting a job, or putting his younger brothers or sisters through school, clearly acting as a substitute for his absent father. If Kawanaka had stopped going to school as a way of becoming dependent on his mother, he was feeling the contradiction of resenting his father and yet taking on the same role in the family. He tried to get rid of this dependence, but tensions arose, and we can view the reason as being that it was not his own dependence on his mother that he was trying to shed but the dependence the father who lived on his mind had practiced. We can understand his stated desire to kill his father as meaning that he wants to kill the part of him that is the same as his father, namely, his dependence on his mother.

Thus, values that arise out of family structures are not individual moods or feelings. However, those values are a dynamic that permeates the entire family and becomes a system that maintains the family structure, a whirlpool of energy that works more forcefully than any individual. People can become aware of their individual feelings so they can choose to express them or not, and they find it easy to control these feelings simply through their own will.

However, feelings that arise out of family systems cannot be changed by individual will, because they are living things that are born out of the family system as a whole. Unless the entire family becomes aware of the mechanisms and values of that system and tries to change them, the system will continue to operate like a perpetual motion machine.

Chapter Three: What Does "Transgenerational" Mean?

3.1 Families Are a Refuge for the Heart

Case 9: The Girl Who Found Her Way to Her Hometown

One day, I was talking with a public health nurse, a woman in her forties who was working in her home region of Tohoku, the northern part of the main island of Honshu. She had found work here in accordance with her parents' wishes, and our talk concerned the first time she had felt the joy of working.

During her first year as a visiting nurse for the city government, she received a message from a household in the district she was in charge of. The message said, "There's some sort of creature living in a house in our neighborhood." The reference was to a house where a very elderly couple had lived. The man had died several years ago, his widow had died about a year before, and the house was standing empty.

When this nurse peeked into the house, she caught a fleeting glimpse of a black shadow. The thought that it might be a stray dog came to mind, but she wondered how a stray dog could have gotten into the house, and anyway, why would it? She stood in the entryway and called out, but there didn't seem to be anyone inside. She went back to the front yard of the house and opened a glass window that faced the yard.

As she made her way into the house one step at a time, she heard a slight rustling noise, so she went to the room where the noise came from. There she saw a black shadow make a sudden movement as if it had sensed her and was trying to hide. She wondered if some kind of wild animal had wandered in. As stealthily as possible, she proceeded into the room where the unknown shadow had fled.

Slowly opening the door, she found the black shadow crouching inside the dark room. As she approached it, the creature scampered away on all fours to hide. But that black shadow wasn't a dog; it was a woman.

The nurse gasped and gave a startled cry. But the black shadow, still on all fours, hurried to hide in the closet. It looked like a black spider; as if a four-legged spider woman had gone and hidden in the closet.

The nurse spoke to the shadow in a soothing voice. "It's all right. You don't have to be afraid."

Later, the nurse learned of this woman's actual situation. She and her younger brother were the children of the couple who had owned the house. Apparently, the parents had become ill and unable to take care of the children, so the children had been sent to live with relatives. The boy was given to a local relative, one of his mother's siblings, but the girl was sent far away to western Japan, near Osaka. At that time, the children were still in elementary school, with the boy in first grade and the girl in second or third grade.

The nurse was unable to find out exactly what had happened to the children after that, but neither of them had ever lived in that house with their parents again.

At the time the nurse found her, the woman was already grown up, and no one knew how long she had lived with her foster parents in western Japan. However, her appearance gave a hint of the cruel circumstances she must have experienced over the years. At some point, she had begun moving around on all fours.

It was surmised that she had been kept in some sort of closet or storage shed. She may have been fed like an animal or given hardly any space to move around in. The fact that she moved around on all fours gave a clue to the kind of life she had been forced to live.

Yet how had she been able to return to her old home? What sorts of reasons led her to do this? Maybe her relatives in western Japan heard that her parents were dead and stopped taking care of her, or maybe they threw her out of the house sometime before that. Either way, how had she made her way from faraway western Japan to the northern reaches of the island of Honshu?

This woman was eventually put into an institution, and the nurse visited that institution some six months later. Through the window, she could see the woman sitting quietly and calmly in the garden, with a peaceful expression on her face. The nurse was pleased to see the gentle posture and calm face the woman projected.

Hearing the story of the children's fate broke my heart, but the question of how the woman had made her way from western Japan to the far north kept going round and round in my head. I remember being preoccupied with thinking about it.

The fact that she was caked with dirt indicated she had been out of contact with other people for a long time. She was probably unable to talk to anyone in an unfamiliar area. Even if she had sneaked onto an overnight train and hidden, other passengers would have spotted her. Even if she had somehow hidden among the cargo of a truck, how had she reached her destination? At that time, transportation was not as well developed as it is now, so perhaps it took her half a year to travel the distance. Or maybe it took her several years. What was she thinking as she set out alone to find the home of her parents, where she had been born and brought up in her early childhood?

What struck me in all this was that people want to "return to the place where they were born" when something happens.

Even with the horrible life she had led, the refuge for her heart was her family. It may be that we humans have an animalistic instinct of wanting to return to wherever our family is. No matter what environment people are placed in, their family landscape serves as a guide for living.

Whenever I think about the theme of "families," I can't help recalling this story. Families are dynamic forces that draw their members in, entities that reach beyond time and space.

3.2 Transgenerational Effects

Negative Transgenerational Effects from Generation to Generation

I first experienced transgenerational effects at a session conducted by Dr. Paula Bottome (1934-2001) about twenty-five years ago. At that point, I had not yet internalized the concept of "transgenerational effects."

A certain man was participating in a therapy group on the Japanese island of Kyushu. At that time, I was Paula's interpreter, and I did not yet entirely understand what psychological therapy was, but I did know that her kindly approach appealed to me. I was also very interested in Carl Rogers' style of gentle dialogue therapy.

The man told Paula about the counseling he had received, and that this counseling had helped him a great deal. What prompted him to receive counseling was, in his words, "An impulse that came out of nowhere, one I don't know the reason for, that kept telling me that I wanted to die. When that kind of energy welled up within me, I thought that I needed help from somebody, so I underwent counseling."

I was still an eager beginner in all this, so I was surprised to hear the words "end my life" and "I want to die" from a client. I shuddered inwardly at the thought of how such a situation would play out.

Paula focused on a certain energy in him, a kind of nervous affect that possessed him against his will, the desire to die that welled up inside him. She told the man to feel the full force of that energy. Within a matter of twenty minutes, he was able to extract that lump of energy from the depths of his belly.

He said that it was like a black lump of iron, a symbol of the tensions that his family retained. "All my family does is fight," he said. "My siblings and I are all adults, but we still fight. My relatives argue. I think this lump comes from the fact that my parents and my other relatives do nothing but fight." He seemed calmer and more settled than before.

His manner of speaking became more relaxed as he continued. "This isn't just something that happens in the current generation of my family. This thing that looks like a black lump is a problem that my mother and father inherited from their parents. My grandfather and grandmother also fought a lot. Now all the people in my extended family hate one another. I'm going to make it stop in my own generation." His family had been prominent in the region for ages, but it had also transmitted a chain of hatred from generation to generation.

After I encountered this situation, I formed an image in my mind of some kind of black substance, a negative legacy that had been transmitted through the generations. I began to wonder how this "lump of black iron" had been passed down from ancestors to descendants, from the previous generation to the new generation, from the former family to the new family, from today's parents to their children. Something invisible to everyone is certainly being passed down to the next generation. How does the new generation receive this invisible message? By what means is it transmitted?

At that point, I had not yet discovered the answers to that question. However, when I became familiar with Gestalt therapy, I began to ask myself, "What if the emotional problems that a client is conflicted about are not that client's own problems, but **unresolved** emotional problems passed down through the generations among the members of the client's family?"

It then became possible for clients to change their point of view and think, "This is not my problem but a family problem that I inherited." I saw with my own eyes that most individuals' problems disappeared in the process of doing the work. That's why I decided to investigate the **unresolved** problems that are the basis of transgenerational effects.

And then, in the northern region of Tohoku, I had to deal with nearly the same long-term problem again, a problem having to do with family quarrels. However, it was not the person troubled by family quarrels who came to see me; it was his wife. She was originally from Osaka and had moved to Tohoku after getting married some ten years before.

Case 10: A Multigenerational Tradition of Quarreling at Family Gatherings

The woman's husband was a serious and responsible person, and she reported that their relationship was "just like that of any other family." The couple had two children. The way the woman explained the problem was, "My husband was fretting about the Takenaka family and became depressed. He's gotten over it and gone back to work, but during the time he was depressed, he received counseling and became interested in psychological therapy."

She began the session by explaining that she had come to me for advice about the problems of the Takenaka family. She stated that her husband had recovered from his depression but that the source of his depression, the problems of the Takenaka family, had not been solved at all. The family included five siblings, of which her husband was the eldest. The siblings got together once a month for what might be called a social gathering. The families of the various siblings, including their children, participated in these gatherings, so they were almost like little family reunions.

"The problem is the quarrels that occur at those parties," she said. According to her, some family member invariably became the target of everyone else's criticisms, with insults flying back and forth: "It's your fault! You're the problem!" Her husband found these sessions to be exhausting, and that was the cause of his depression.

"I feel that there's something odd about it," she remarked. "This Takenaka family may have the same family name as a famous samurai, but their family tree isn't all that distinguished."

The other members of the group laughed at her comment, but she continued talking.

"It's odd that the whole family, every single one of them, shows up for these 'fight clubs' every time. It's as if they enjoy them. I really don't feel like taking our children to these gatherings where their relatives are fighting all the time. I've told my husband about not wanting to take the children along, but I can't make him understand. He knows what I'm saying, but he insists that these are important gatherings, so we have to take the children. I really can't understand this."

Then, about six months later, her husband came with her to participate in a session. His conversations with his wife had motivated him to want to know what was going on in the Takenaka family.

He spoke about his parents, and we learned that his parents had also quarreled constantly with him and his siblings. In other words, his parents had acted the same way. His wife, who had come from distant Osaka to marry into the family, was able to look at the "fight club" objectively and see that they were odd. However, since the husband had grown up in the Takenaka family, with his parents' generation continually quarreling, he didn't think there was anything wrong with it.

According to the husband, his grandparents' generation had been equally quarrelsome. Even though his wife seemed surprised at this family tradition, he himself had just accepted it as normal.

The gatherings felt like the "struggle sessions" of Maoist China in that each time, a different person was chosen to be the target of everyone else's criticism. Of course, none of the people involved were consciously aware of what they were doing.

Once the husband understood this three-generation "family tradition," he agreed that he would not take the children to these gatherings anymore.

Thus, the people involved were unaware that they were part of a "fight club." Far from it: they thought they were just carrying on a tradition of gatherings that had begun in their parents' generation. They didn't even acknowledge that what they did during these gatherings was fight. As the eldest son, the serious and responsible husband had felt that refereeing the fights was his duty, and he had taken the task seriously, which was the source of his exhaustion. He had also been the victim of transgenerational negativity.

3.3 Anger Across Generations

Case 11: Love Lay Behind the Anger

A man in his thirties told me, "I'm troubled by my anger." He looked like a very mild-mannered, kindly type, so this seemed hard to believe. According to him, he was able to talk to his work colleagues and friends calmly and reasonably. Yet when it came to his family, he reacted emotionally.

I didn't get the impression that he was guilty of any domestic violence. He said, "Even when my work colleagues or friends express an opinion or idea that is different from mine, I'm able to discuss it with them calmly." However, any irritation he felt exploded into rage when he was at home. "I end up yelling at my wife," he admitted. His anger was also directed at his children, and he spoke roughly to them. Even he was disturbed by the imbalance between the way he acted toward outsiders and the way he acted toward his family.

After one outburst, his elementary-school-aged daughter told him, "I hate you when you're angry all the time!" He had not expected her to say that, and it really shook him to the core.

However, the real reason he was disturbed was that he had repeated those same words to himself in reference to his mother. Ever since he was a child, his home had continually been filled with the sound of his mother yelling at his father. Looking at her, he would silently scream, "I hate you when you're angry all the time."

About two months later, his mother came to participate in one of the counseling sessions. She actually seemed pained at her own habit of yelling at her husband and letting her emotions boil over into anger. She looked as if she was in her sixties and gave the impression of being a powerhouse at work, someone to be reckoned with on the job. Her husband had already retired, and at the thought that she would soon retire and have to spend every day together with him, she wanted to do something about her anger.

So I turned to her and said, "I want to see what you're like when you're angry." She said, "I couldn't do that," but she still stood up. I then had her imagine she was facing her husband and had her yell, "What are you doing?!" She certainly had an overwhelming presence when she was angry. I had her shout several more times:

"What are you doing?"

As she continued shouting, her voice broke, as if she were about to burst into tears. She took a deep breath. Then, as if trying to calm herself, she said, "I want to stop doing this." Still on the verge of tears, she added, "Even so, the anger wells up from deep inside me, and I end up yelling."

Something nagged at me as I observed the situation. She had imagined her husband to be quite a long way away. When I asked her the reason, she said, "He's always shutting himself away in his den." Yet it looked to me as if she was shouting at someone even farther away.

When this woman yelled at her husband, she also cried, doing both things at once. When she yelled, she cried, even though these were conflicting actions. Of course, sometimes people cry when they are angry, but seeing how she looked when she was angry, I felt as if she was yelling more out of sadness than out of anger. The expression on her face seemed to say, "An impulse that I can't stop is welling up inside me." In order to learn more about the two messages her body was sending, I asked her to face in the opposite direction from her husband and start yelling.

She turned around, then back again, and cried out, "Oh, now I get it!"

That's right. She wasn't angry at her husband. She realized that she was yelling at her father: "Stop being so angry!"

When she was in elementary school, her father was always yelling at her mother, and those were the scenes that were awakened in her mind. Her father was a large man and was considered successful in the community, so if everything didn't go exactly the way he wanted, he blamed his wife, who was a gentle person and put up with his behavior. (He may have been able to control his emotions outside the house.) However, witnessing his outbursts every day, my client's mother felt so sorry for her own mother. She recalled a vow she had made to herself as a child:

"When I grow up, I'll get angry (at my father) on behalf of my mother."

However, by the time she was an adult, her father had stopped being such an anger junkie and was kind to her mother. She got married and left home and forgot about the unpleasantness that had occurred during her childhood. Yet when her husband got to be the same age that her father had been during his angry period, he began to elicit her rage. Her husband had always been kind to her, and despite her angry outbursts, she had never thought of leaving or divorcing him.

At that point, I remembered a passage from Bert Hellinger's *Love's Own Truth: Bonding and Balancing in Close Relationships* (2001):

"When a family has problems, those are not problems but situations that are complications of love," or something to that effect. I remember being deeply moved by these words.

We try to solve a family's problems as if they were just **problems**, but that is not where the solutions are to be found. **They are not problems; they are just complications of love.**

In this case, this woman thought on a daily basis that she wanted to prevent her father from yelling at her mother in an authoritarian and high-handed way. This was the dynamic of a child who loved her mother, distressed at the way her father took advantage of her mother and emotionally abused her. The mother may have been silently crying out to her daughter for help. However, even if a mere elementary-school girl like her could have inferred what her mother was thinking, she could not protect her from her big hulk of a father. She found this situation extremely painful.

At some point, she began thinking, "When I grow up, I will get angry at him to protect my mother." She repeated this to herself every day. This gave rise to a triangle of anger, in which . . .

(1) Her father raged at her mother.
(2) Her mother silently pleaded for help.
(3) The daughter wanted to help her mother and yell at her father.

However, she unconsciously repressed these feelings, only to have them explode at some time in the future.

A Triangle of Anger

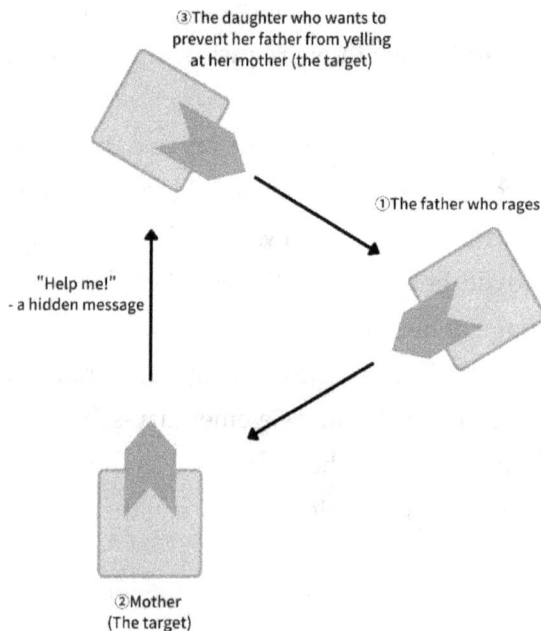

③The daughter who wants to prevent her father from yelling at her mother (the target)

①The father who rages

"Help me!"
- a hidden message

②Mother
(The target)

By the time my client's mother married and left home, relations between her parents had calmed down, so she forget what had happened in her childhood. However, when her husband reached the age her father was during his "anger junkie" period and she herself entered her sixties, an impulsive anger came welling up within her. She had no idea of the meaning of this dynamic, and this pained her. Even though she was the one who was yelling at her husband, she herself was miserable. Her episodes of rage soon dissolved into tears.

As she yelled at her husband, "What are you doing?" and got all choked up, she was unconsciously returning to her childhood. In her frenzy of anger, she was expressing what she was unable to express earlier in life.

The triangle of anger led to a chain of anger in which the men and women exchanged roles each generation. In the first generation, the father rages at the mother. In response, the daughter directs her resentment at her father in order to protect her mother. In the second generation, the daughter becomes a mother and rages at her husband. Seeing this, their son feels sorry for his father and directs his resentment at his mother. Then, in the third generation, the son gets married and begins raging at his wife. The wife signals her unhappiness to her daughter, who starts to resent her father. Thus, the pattern repeats itself.

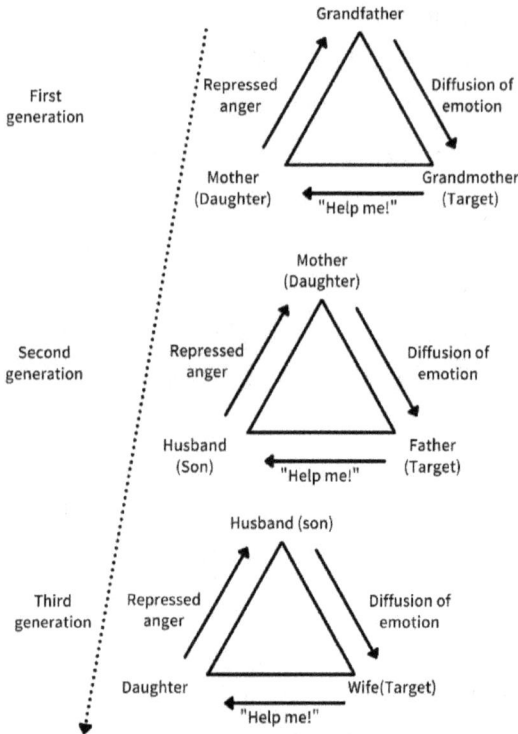

However, we were able to find an opening for solving this transgenerational chain. That was because the daughter in the third-generation family was able to express her feelings to her father: "I hate you when you're angry all the time!" This enabled him (the son of the second generation) to express his thoughts to his mother directly.

In essence, in the third generation, the grandson was able to express what his grandfather had not been able to express. Could that have been a coincidence? Or could it have been that this transgenerational chain was brought to a halt by a system for liberation that is informed by knowledge?

No matter what kind of unfinished business there is, if one member of the family notices what is going on and begins looking for a clue, the chain can be untangled. **When people become aware of the patterns in the family chain reaction, they can put an end to its role in the family dynamics.**

3.4 Family Vectors

Families flow through time from generation to generation, and this sequence of events is like a weight-bearing pillar that maintains the structural integrity of a house; like the skeleton of a house. Pillars like these are invisible to the people who live in the house that contains them. The systems that sustain a family are outside the awareness of the people who live in it, and they pay no attention to these systems.

However, these pillars and crossbeams have a dynamic that works upon each individual member of the family. We might call it a flow of energy, but the people involved rarely notice that this kind of dynamic is affecting them. Even so, it is possible to observe the dynamic and direction of this invisible energy. We will represent this dynamic flow with the word "vector."

Case 12: Feminine Principles and Masculine Principles

Misako Arimura grew up in a typical Japanese family, and what was troubling her was the kind of friction between mothers and children that can be found anywhere. She has an older brother, but relations between the two siblings had frayed, and Misako fretted about the fact they couldn't seem to get close to each other.

I wondered what had happened to the relationship between the mother and the siblings. Where had the low-key conflict between the mother and her two children come from? It welled up out this family like a spring bringing water to the surface. I wanted to find the ultimate source of the spring.

Events in a family are sometimes affected by the people of the previous generation, and sometimes that generation continues to affect the generation after that. These effects continue because the new generation receives and incorporates invisible family vectors without noticing them. These hidden vectors are precisely the source of transgenerational effects.

Until we understand their meanings, the force of the vectors wells up from within the family and continues to exert its influence on each person.

Misako is a systems engineer at an IT corporation, and she is troubled about her relationship with her brother. Even though he is older, he seems overly dependent on their mother. If some problem comes up, he consults their mother. His wife is from a local family. They all live in the historic city of Kyoto, and since Misako's brother felt more secure living near their mother, he decided long ago that he would marry only a "local Kyoto girl."

Misako told me, "I may have been reacting to the way my mother and brother are, but I chose to attend a university in Tokyo. It's not exactly that I had a long-standing desire to leave home, but when I graduated from high school, I decided that I wanted my freedom. My brother got angry and asked, 'Are you going to abandon our mother by going to Tokyo?' That wasn't my intention at all, but it may have been the case that I found my brother's attitude to be stifling. It wasn't so much that I wanted to be free of my mother. It was more that I wanted to liberate myself from my brother's obsessive attachment to our family.

"I'm still single, and I really like Tokyo. Maybe my mother senses this attitude because lately, she's taken to phoning me frequently. She doesn't come out and say it, but she clearly hints that she wants me to move back to Kyoto and look for a job there. She's the type of mother who likes to have her children close by. But the more my mother and brother try to persuade me to move back to Kyoto, the more I want to remain in Tokyo."

I had Misako show me the relationships among the three of them with a "family sculpture," including their relative distance from one another. I was thus able to perceive their relationships clearly in terms of distance.

Me

Brother

Mother

"My brother is close to my mother," she explained. "I feel a bit removed from them. In some ways, I'm separating from them myself. In fact, I consciously moved away from my mother. I don't want her talking at me. Of course, my brother is facing my mother, just like always. I'm not only separate from them, but I am consciously separating myself so I don't have to see them.

"Even so, when I see that my mother and brother are close to each other, I feel lonely, as if I'm all by myself. Actually, if I also went closer to my mother and faced her, just as my brother odes, I don't know how comfortable I would be. For some reason, ever since I was a child, I've felt that I shouldn't do that."

At this point, she started to cry.

When I directed her to indicate the relationship among the three of them, I asked her to portray **distance**. However, I could see that **direction** was a forceful dynamic in the relationships within that family.

Here we find that there are two vectors within a family. When people speak about their own families, the relationships within those families are expressed into terms of the two vectors of **distance** and **direction**.

In this case, there seems to be a deeper meaning to Misako's statement, "I've felt that I shouldn't do that." In order to get a picture of the relationships among all the members of the family, I asked her to add her father to the family sculpture.

Here is what she told me about her father:

"My father doesn't say anything to the rest of us. He just does whatever my mother tells him. He doesn't interact with the rest of us. If I put my father into the family, the three of us become closer. It's always about my mother and us, her children, interacting with each other at home. It may be that my ties to my mother are pretty strong. Since my father is a man, he's not included. My brother is a man too, but ever since he was little, he's clung to my mother."

When I asked Misako about her own relationship with her father, she replied, "I have a close relationship with my father. My brother tells me, 'You have it good.' I was always Dad's favorite, so he'd scold me and say things like 'I just can't talk to Dad.' Ever since I was a child, I was jealous of my brother, so I'd answer him with 'You always depend on Mom for everything.' "

The friction between their parents that had marked the siblings' childhood apparently continued after they became adults. Many people have been called "Daddy's girl" or "Mama's boy" in their childhood, and many children's preferences for one parent or the other can be maintained into adulthood.

Looking at things from the parents' point of view, sometimes parents turn their children into "Daddy's girls" or "Mama's boys." It's a pattern in which the father prefers one of the children, and the mother acts affectionately toward the other. When creating a family sculpture, it is important to portray the two points of view clearly.

In Misako's case, the parents' relationship appears to have designated the children as "Mama's boy" and "Daddy's girl."

We can tell this from the way in which she described the relationship between the siblings. Because her brother always clung to their mother, she had said, "I won't do that."

However, she reported feeling sad and lonely when she saw how close her mother and brother were and the directions they faced. We could interpret that as meaning, "I would like to be in my brother's position." From her brother's words ("You have it good. You're Dad's favorite"), we can observe that both siblings love both their parents.

So could it be that the structure of Misako's family created a dynamic in which her parents each loved only one of their children? If so, where did that dynamic come from?

Could it have come from some past event that no one outside the family knew? Or could it have arisen from the relationship between the two parents? Or could the cause lie in the upbringings of either the father or the mother?

Misako stated that her grandmother's influence was the reason for her father's remaining aloof from the family. "My paternal grandmother has a strong personality," she said, "and since my mother has a strong personality too, they can't get along and are always at odds. They lived together, and the mother-in-law versus daughter-in-law conflicts were fierce. When those two started arguing, Dad couldn't get a word in edgewise."

It was as if Misako had already devised a basic model of her father's behavior. "He doesn't get involved in women's conflicts. He's like a mosquito outside the mosquito net." From the very beginning of Misako's parents' marriage, her father had been forced out of intervening in the conflicts between his strong-willed mother and his strong-willed wife. Of course, he may have chosen to stay out of these quarrels on his own.

A Proxy War Between the Mother and Grandmother

The relationships among the parents and children and between the siblings that form the present-day family have their source in things that happened before Misako and her brother were born.

In cases like this, where there is a high level of conflict between a mother-in-law and a daughter-in-law, the firstborn child may become a tool in the war between the two. If the mother-in-law is the more powerful figure, she naturally takes control of the child and uses that child as an ally in her efforts to control the family. It is understandable that the child's mother does not want to allow her mother-in-law to do this, so a "war" with hidden tactics arises to decide who has the right to shower that child with love. A dynamic arises in which the grandmother wants to be the one who dotes on the child. In opposition to that, the mother maneuvers to be the one who is the child's principal source of love. In other words, the child becomes an object of contention in a proxy war between two adults.

In the case of Misako's family, the first child was a boy, and Misako's mother was the stronger party here. This is clear from the positions of her mother and brother in the family sculpture that I had her create. Misako's mother was determined not to hand her son over to her mother-in-law, so she stood in front of him to guard him. In a sense, Misako's brother was always forced to look at his mother's back.

Misako's mother may have asked her husband, who did not protect her from his own mother, not to take her side. We can infer this from Misako's statement that "[My father] just does whatever my mother tells him." Yet her father also has his own viewpoint. Since he most likely does not hate his own mother, he may have chosen to be "a mosquito outside the mosquito netting" and not get involved in the conflicts between the two women. In any case, I will discuss his situation below.

This is the process for the women of the family, the flow of their energy, what we might call the women's family vectors. As a man, Misako's father is inevitably excluded from the women's vector. This is only natural and even an extremely healthy development.

The mother takes care to protect her son (Misako's brother) from his grandmother by making sure that he is always behind her. The natural result is that the son sticks close to his mother and is always near her. This relationship is very satisfying to the mother and follows naturally from the circumstances.

The Women's Vector

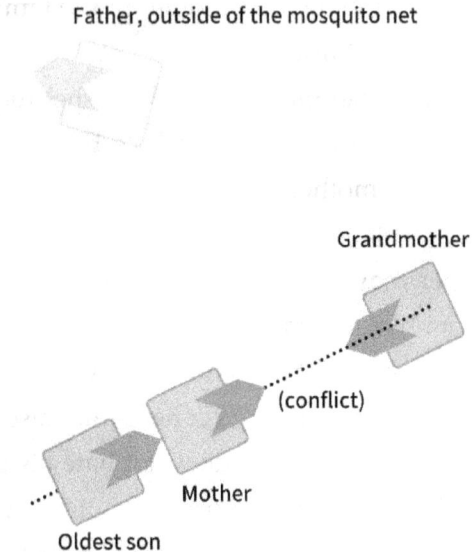

Father, outside of the mosquito net

Grandmother

(conflict)

Mother

Oldest son

So what happened when the second child, Misako, was born? Instead of letting her mother-in-law take charge of Misako, she made sure that the child was close to her father. If the grandmother's dynamic is the strongest force in the family, the first child can become "Grandma's baby." In this case, Misako's mother was the stronger person, so she did not allow this to happen. Even so, she had no inner resources left for a second child. It would have been a natural development for the second child to become "Grandma's baby" in a place and time that the mother could not reach. Fortunately, Misako's father always did what his wife told him to, and she kept sending him hidden messages that said, "I want you to take care of our daughter."

Since Misako's father loved his wife, that's what he did. In that way, the second child drew closer to her father instead of closer to her grandmother.

Her brother's words, "You have it good, being able to sit on Dad's lap," are an expression of this result. Misako sat on her father's lap, not her grandmother's, a result that was also satisfying for her mother.

It was not only the mother's forceful personality that made this result possible. Paradoxically, the grandmother's status as a strong woman also helped create this situation. The grandmother gave birth to her son, Misako's father, soon after she was married. However, her husband, Misako's grandfather, became ill and died soon after his son was born. In order to preserve the family business, the grandmother took over her late husband's work and ran the business and the household efficiently. Only her inner strength enabled her to do this. Or it may be that she had to become strong in order to survive. In any case, the grandmother fulfilled the roles of both mother and father for her son.

Having been raised by such a strong woman, Misako's father wanted his wife to be capable of both superior inner strength and deep affection. Once we understood this relationship, the broad outlines of the meaning of Misako's conflict began to emerge faintly.

At this point, I'm not trying to show how the relationship between the mother and the two children developed. Instead, I want to use the minor conflicts between the siblings to show the relations between the parents and how relationships in the previous generations affected them in subtle ways. These influences were different in each family, and there was no single pattern or tendency that accounts for these effects. I will show you examples of how invisible generational dynamics were at work in each family.

So why was the grandmother, who was supposed to be strong, so satisfied? Because the oldest son had become a mama's boy, while the second child, had become a daddy's girl. Either of them might have become "Grandma's pet." In order to understand this, let's take a look at the situation in terms of vectors.

Dynamics exist within a family, and they are represented in physical form by vectors. If we view the relations in a family in terms of the two vectors (dynamics) of distance and direction, lines emerge that link the generations. The two transgenerational vectors are alive within the **here** and **now** of the family. Misako's brother is on his grandmother and mother's female line, while Misako is on her grandmother's (and grandfather's) and father's male line. The grandmother stands opposite Misako's mother as a female vector. However, she is satisfied because her grandson (Misako's older brother) is flowing on that vector. (See the following diagram.)

Male Vector

Misako

Father

Father's role

Grandmother

Mother's role

Female Vector

Mother

Older brother

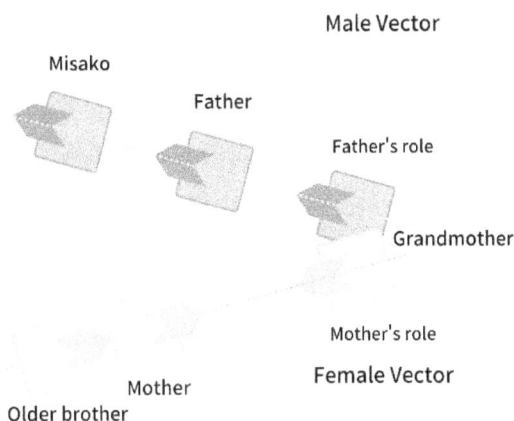

The grandmother took over the grandfather's family business. She is satisfied because both Misako and her father are on that vector. The placement of her two grandchildren on two lines accomplished the role of linking the generations. On the female vector, the generations are linked through Misako's brother. On the male vector, the generations are linked through Misako, and the grandmother is satisfied with this state of affairs.

If Misako could have been on her mother's vector, there might have been no conflict between the siblings. If she had been born a boy, the natural course of events would have occurred. But that is all speculation. It is sufficient to know that Misako's family is affected by invisible transgenerational vectors from the grandparents.

So what does it mean when someone is on an extension of a vector? Misako's brother is on an extension of the vector of his mother, who is facing his grandmother. His grandmother sees him as an enemy, not consciously or with any understanding, but with an animal-like instinct. Since Misako's mother placed her son on the vector of her mother-in-law, who stands facing her, so she instinctively feels as if she is shielding him from the gaze of the grandmother who hates him. In other words, to protect her son, she has increasingly moved him to a position behind her. Put in sports terms, she has set up what is known as a defensive line and an offensive line.

Misako's grandmother often spoke critically to her son about his wife, but since he loved his wife, he didn't say anything about it to either of them. He placed himself completely outside the conflict between the two women—a very wise move, I think. On the other hand, Misako is on an extension of her father's vector, and he dotes on her. As she expressed it once she became aware of the fact, "I was a girl, so I could sit on my father's lap."

Being on extensions of two different vectors, the brother and sister do not come into contact with each other. Their grandfather's vector is based on male principles, which move from the family of origin to the outside world. That is why Misako longed for the world outside her family.

The grandmother's vector, even for people who are standing in opposition to her, is based on female principles, based on staying within a cohesive family group. Thus, Misako's brother, located on the female vector, has chosen to remain within the family framework.

It is fair to assume that the brother and sister—placed on different vectors, the two vectors present in the family—are living according to principles that comprise two different views of life.

In his 2007 book *Integral Spirituality*, American philosopher Ken Wilber (born 1949) has described these two vectors as **masculine principles** and **feminine principles**. He states that masculinity implies agency: that it is a tendency toward autonomy and an orientation toward the outside world. Femininity implies communion: that is commonality, interaction, and sensitivity, so their awareness is directed toward the community known as the family.

The table below describes the masculine and feminine principles that human beings have. These two principles coexist inside individuals. Rather than saying men have masculine principles and women have feminine principles, it is more accurate to say that both principles are at work inside individual human beings. These principles are transmitted to children within the family.

In general, it is fair to say that mothers transmit feminine principles to their daughters and fathers transmit masculine principles to their sons. However, at the same time, fathers also transit feminine principles to their daughters, and mothers transmit masculine principles to their sons. It is not even unusual for mothers to run the family based on masculine principles, or for fathers to have a more feminine core and to live their lives on that basis.

Masculine principles/Examples of masculine characteristics	Feminine principles/ Examples of feminine characteristics
• Agency (autonomy, independence)	• Communion (relatedness, links)
• Order (organization)	• Chaos
• Yang	• Yin
• Strictness	• Kindness
• Toughness	• Softness
• Rationality (Logical nature)	• Irrationality (instinctiveness)
• Philosophical	• Emotional
• Ethics of correct behavior (self-control, correct behavior, rights)	• Ethics of care (relatedness, consideration, sense of responsibility)
• Dualism	• Monism (objectivity)
• Structure	• Lack of structure
• Vertical	• Horizontal
• Paternalism	• Maternalism

Aoki, Kubota, Koda, and Suzuki. "Introduction to Integral Theory" [Integuraru riron nyuumon 1]. Shunjuusha, 2010, p. 139.

In any case, within families, the parents teach their children, either consciously or unconsciously, the principles that they should live by, both masculine principles and feminine principles. These approaches differ depending on the relationship between the parents and are also affected by the relationship between any grandparents who happen to live in the household.

It is only natural that the balance among the members of a family should change in subtle ways. The children in each new generation grow up absorbing these principles from their parents' generation, but how they understand these principles can be significantly affected by their nation and its communities, the era they find themselves in, or their religion and culture.

Chapter Four: The Theoretical Background of Transgenerational Therapy

4.1 What is Gestalt Therapy?

Gestalt therapy is a practical method of psychological therapy invented by the psychiatrist Frederick S. Perls and his wife, Gestalt psychologist Laura Perls. By practical, we mean that it is **a method centered on the here and now**, without analysis or interpretation of the client's past or upbringing.

One of the theoretical elements of Gestalt therapy is Gestalt psychology, a type of experimental psychology that concerns a person's awareness of the world. Part of the definition lies in the fundamental concept of *Gestalt*, which means "overall form" or "that which cannot be divided." A person's awareness of the world comes about when he or she becomes aware of a meaningful Gestalt.

When I recognize you, I do not recognize only the various individual parts of your body, such as your arms, legs, torso, facial expression, stomach, or heart. I recognize you as a whole entity, a Gestalt. In the same way, we treat a person's mind and body as a single Gestalt, without splitting them from each other.

Gestalt therapy is also a psychological therapy that focuses on *awareness.* **Awareness occurs when a person is aware of the world.** Humans are not the only creatures with this capacity. Plants and animals are able to become aware of what they need to stay alive. Plants extend their roots into the soil to obtain nutrients. That is because they can seek out the directions in which nutrient elements and water lie. Above the ground, they grow leaves and new buds to face the sun because they have acquired the ability to recognize the bright sunlight.

Animals have even more complicated abilities to notice things. When they feel hungry, animals act to find food. At such times, they employ their five senses (sight, hearing, smell, taste, and touch) to notice what they need. From early childhood, humans notice when their throats and lips are dry, and they know that they need water. If they need to find a supply of water, they can take action to do so.

Fritz and Laura Perls classified awareness into three zones. The first is the **outer zone.** You are able to use your five senses to be aware of the real world outside your own body. The second is the **inner zone,** which is concerned with awareness of what is happening inside you, including in your mind. You are aware of your own body's pain, breathing, hunger, joy, tiredness, or other feelings, and you act or express yourself to form Gestalt— that is, to complete that which is insufficient. The third zone is the **middle zone,** awareness of your thoughts; that is, the functions of your brain. It is thanks to these functions that humanity has created civilizations and cultures.

A special characteristic of Gestalt therapy is that **it treats the body and the mind as one entity**. Human beings never exist as two separate parts, the body and the mind.

For example, if you are suffering from some kind of mental anxiety, your muscles, perhaps the ones in your shoulders or neck, perhaps the muscles that control breathing, tense up. When you are sad, you cry, and tears flow. On the other hand, when you tense your body, your mind feels unstable, giving rise to anxiety, anger, insomnia, irritability, or other psychological phenomena. When clients talk about their problems, the therapist pays attention not only to their words or expressions but also to **what they are expressing with their bodies, here and now.**

The Gestalt therapy approach is also a method of taking the things that we have split ourselves off from—conflicts with other people and the things that have cut us off from our own emotions—and integrating them into a whole picture; in other words, forming a Gestalt.

To explain how *awareness* works in Gestalt therapy, Perls used the concepts of *figure* and *ground*. To demonstrate this, an illustration showing two rows of five Rubin glasses is often provided. Sometimes, when you look at this, you may see goblets on a shelf; other times, what you perceive is a row of faces.

However, it is impossible for you to see both goblets and faces at the same time. If you are looking at the goblets, you can't see the faces, and if you are looking at the faces, you can't see the goblets. You end up seeing whichever one you are more interested in at the moment. As your interest fades, you seek a new stimulus, and a new object of awareness appears.

I have explained awareness using this principle. The part of the drawing that comes to the foreground is the *figure*, and it tends to be the one that people need at the time. The other figure, the one that one cannot currently see, is called the *ground*.

In Gestalt therapy, things that are drawing our attention (either the goblets or the faces, for example) are called *figures*, while things that recede into the background and out of our attention when we receive a new stimulus are called *grounds*.

When people are hungry, food is the foremost thought in their minds, and their attention turns to lunch, with thoughts like, "I'd like to have ramen noodles today" or "I think I'll go to that restaurant." At that point, their work or whatever they were searching on the internet recedes into the background and becomes a *ground*.

Yet once they've eaten lunch, a new thought comes to mind — "I could use a cup of coffee" — so their attention turns to looking for a coffee shop. Whatever they had for lunch has left them satisfied, so it also becomes a *ground*. They naturally head for a familiar chain coffee shop, and once they're inside, they look at the menu, and thoughts about what kind of coffee they want occupy their mind and become a *figure*.

After a while, a new idea for work comes to mind. You think, "That's an interesting idea," and you want to get up and leave. At that point, images of that interesting idea for work, and of the people who may be connected with it, become the *figures*. Coffee is no longer on your mind, and it becomes a *ground*.

Awareness is also a conscious process. Moment by moment, things that you need or things or the things that draw your physical or emotional interest become the focus of your awareness.

Unfinished business is always a *figure*, and it rises to the upper levels of consciousness. This continues until the matter is concluded. I will explain more about this unfinished business — that is, these unresolved problems — later, but it is important to understand how they are connected with transgenerational issues.

Four Pillars for Understanding Transgenerational Issues

Contemporary Gestalt therapy has incorporated several theoretical underpinnings. In order to help you understand the topic of transgenerational issues, I'd like to present four theoretical concepts: field theory, family sculpture, unresolved problems, and physical memory.

How do families look when viewed in terms of these theories? I'd like to explain how psychology and psychotherapy understand intergenerational transmission and transgenerational issues.

What kinds of characteristics do the groups that we call families have? Unique psychological factors arise in families, and there are relationships within families, or in other words, systems that maintain the family. So how are we supposed to understand these systems? There have been many attempts to devise theories about them in terms of sociology, anthropology, or psychology.

We can think of the family as a building supported by pillars in the form of the following theories, which are essential for understanding transgenerational issues.

The first pillar is **field theory**. It is used to describe in an easily understandable way how human relations are intertwined with one another in the unique space we call the family. It is a theory that considers the invisible magnetic fields that members of a family or any other group share with one another

The second pillar is **family sculpture**. This approach makes it possible to represent family relationships visually. One of its techniques, the **empty chair technique**, is widely used in a variety of counseling methods. It gets its name from the practice of telling the client to imagine family members sitting in a chair and to have a conversation with them.

The third pillar is **unresolved problems**, a theory unique to Gestalt therapy. This theory involves bringing the client's unresolved feelings and experiences to the surface in order to solve them. Otherwise, they may continue plaguing the client, irrespective of time or space.

Unresolved problems are also a system by which unfinished business is transmitted from generation to generation. The therapist focuses on this unfinished business in search of clues to solving the problems.

The fourth pillar is looking at **physical memory systems**. In recent years, it has become common for therapists in the North American and European therapy communities to pay attention to their client's bodies to learn about what is going on in their hearts. The reason is that the therapist may not be able to perceive what is happening deep inside the client simply by listening to the client's words. Therapists have come to understand that by paying attention to facial expressions, gestures, tone of voice, posture, and actions (not just listening to the client's words), the therapist can receive **nonverbal messages** from the client. **This leads to a philosophical question:** If we understand families as groups with a single personality, how does the family's physical communication come into being?

Family structures in Japan rest upon these four pillars, but if the framework of the family is these four pillars, then they must be linked by crossbeams. Without these crossbeams, which consist of the theorems and principles that strengthen the pillars and create links among them, the family is unable to withstand the slightest tremor.

So how can we use the four theories to understand the principles and dynamics that transgenerational issues produce? Do they provide clues for solving transgenerational issues? I will begin by taking a look at field theory.

4.2 Field Theory
(Levin's Group Dynamics)

A family is made up of members who share a specific space. Members of the family act as they wish, but they act, behave, and form human relationships not only according to their own will but also according to their individual emotions and moods.

This is because each person has an individual path toward personal growth.

However, invisible familial influences operate in the background like **magnetic fields**. Sometimes, individuals act while thinking that the influences from these invisible magnetic fields are what they themselves want. At this point, I want to discuss how the workings of the magnetic fields create the specific space of the family.

In recent years, Gestalt therapy has reached a third stage as it spreads from the United States to Australia, France, Germany, and other countries, which by itself has led to the development of several theoretical constructs. One of these is **field theory**.

Field theory was first proposed by the Gestalt psychology researcher Kurt Levin (1890-1947). He became world-famous for researching **group dynamics**, a practical field of psychology that tries to figure out the dynamics of groups by researching their norms, decision-making procedures, goals, and structures. In other words, he tried to explain the principles of group dynamics that form the background of individual psychological dynamics.

However, Levin noticed that individuals' emotions are strongly influenced by the groups they belong to. That is because human beings do not exist as individuals but in relation to families, workplaces, religious groups, local communities, and other groups.

Until then, psychology was focused mainly on the growth of the individual or on the psychological processes of individuals. Psychology and psychiatry were fields that explored the individual's psyche to understand emotional problems, to the extent that it would have been fair to call them "individual psychology."

As time went on, Levin's results suggested that the factors behind individuals' relationships, motivations, and demands lie in the group they belong to. Levin's research into group dynamics led to the concept of **life space**.

In other words, Levin broke away from the concept of previous forms of psychology, which tried to explain everything in terms of the individual's unconscious drives and physiological and sexual drives, and proposed a new way of looking at an individual's interactions with his or her environment: the idea that humans act based on motivations and desires that arise in relation to the groups that they belong to.

For that reason, psychologists began to consider the necessity of moving away from individual psychology to a focus on group psychology, or **group dynamics**.

In the human potential movement, which arose in California in the 1960s, Carl Rogers created encounter groups, while Abraham Harold Maslow pointed out that once people's physical needs are met, they start wanting to seek social connections, personal growth, and self-fulfillment. He was one of the founders of **transpersonal psychology**.

With concepts of Gestalt therapy in the air during that same period, it is only natural that there were moves to incorporate groups, societies, and cultures into psychology. Particularly important were Levin's field theory and the incorporation of new viewpoints about groups.

What is a magnetic field?

The **magnetic field theory** is employed as a way of understanding group processes. To understand what a magnetic field is, try imagining the following:

First, imagine sand spread evenly over a sheet of white paper. Then assume that this is not just ordinary sand but sand with iron filings mixed in.

What happens if we pass a magnet over (or under) the piece of paper?

I'm sure many of you remember this experiment or one like it from your elementary-school days. The iron filings are attracted to the direction where the magnet is placed, and they clump up there. By placing the magnet on the paper, you change the way the iron filings are distributed on the paper. The magnet pulls them in with an invisible force.

If we put two more magnets on top of (or under) the paper, the magnetic field changes, and depending on the strength of the second magnet relative to the first one, the iron filings move to two different places. If we add a third and then a fourth magnet, the iron filings change their positions relative to one another until we reach equilibrium, based on the laws of dynamics.

If the iron filings are mixed in with a large amount of sand; you may not be able to see the effects of the magnets. However, if you lift one of the magnets off the paper, the iron filings rise up like a thread following the magnet and adhere to it.

Even though you cannot see the magnetic field on the surface, there are forces at work that draw the iron filings that lie between the various magnets, based on the strength of each magnet.

In field theory, each person is thought of as a magnet. If we consider each family as a specific group, the individual forms his or her own field within a specific space.

Relationships among individuals are maintained by invisible magnetic energy. The greater the force a magnet exerts, the greater the power it has to attract iron filings. Even a small magnet can exert a greater force than a large magnet, depending on its degree of magnetism. The magnetism that these magnets exert on one another is invisible to the human eye. Similarly, it is impossible to take an objective view of the emotional attractions that play a role in relationships among family members.

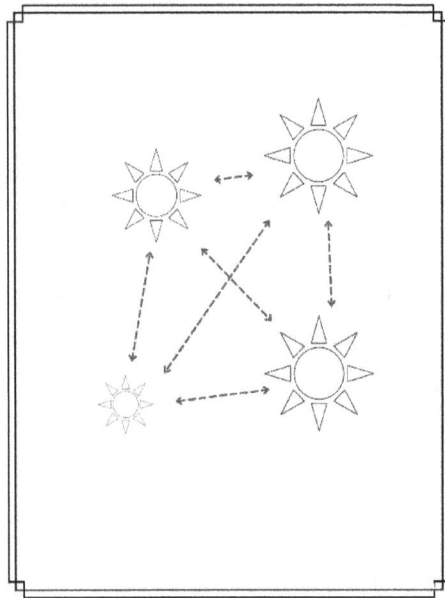

Family members are linked by magnetic fields

Despite that, the family creates relationships while detecting the interactions of the invisible magnetic fields. These concepts are based on Levin's field theory, but he did not come up with them. Field theory is actually a concept from physics, a classical electromagnetic theory first propounded in nineteenth-century Britain by physicist Michael Faraday (1791-1867) and further developed by physicist James Maxwell (1831-1879) .

Levin attempted to explain group dynamics and human relations, environments, and connections among groups using the concepts of field theory. He understood human actions as **varying in relation to their environments**, giving rise to their motivations and desires in a process of evolving changes.

Gestalt therapy has tried to understand groups and families, workplaces and culture, and societal trends in terms of field theory.

What I am trying to do here is look at field theory in terms of transgenerational theory. I want to show how various individual tensions are products of the "field" known as the family.

So how does this family system make use of these magnetic fields, consciously or unconsciously?

In order to understand what is going on, we need to learn about the principles and natural laws that support this theory. We will express these in the form of theorems. Since we have not yet accumulated clinical data to the extent that these principles and laws indicate, we will express matters in flexible terms.

Theorem 1: Spaces Contain Fixed Positions

The members of a family have "places to sit" in their shared space. Consider the image entitled "Family members are linked by their magnetic fields," which depicts a space in which the positions of the four members of a family are determined by the strength or weakness of their magnetic fields. If one magnet has a strong magnetic field, it has a powerful ability to attract other magnets. There are also magnets that exert a counterforce that repels other magnets.

We can view the relationship between parents and children— or between males and females—in terms of the power of magnetic fields. It is also possible to represent the strength of an individual's emotions of joy, anger, sorrow, or pleasure. These magnetic fields and their degrees of intensity may also be seen as representations of people's outward appearance or internal characteristics, views of life, or values.

In any case, **as a result of the equilibrium brought about by these invisible magnetic fields, the members of the family each assume their natural position**s.

Theorem 2: Roles Emerge in Specific Fields

In this specific space full of magnetic fields, various roles develop for the purpose of maintaining the family.

The parents perform the role of raising the children. For their part, the children perform their role of acting like children. The men direct their focus to the world outside the home in order to provide for the women and children, according to masculine principles. In ancient times, men performed this role by hunting for food or fighting to protect their tribe from enemies. Women direct their focus to matters inside the home to take care of the family, according to the feminine principle. They do the cooking and housework and take care of communication within the family.

These roles arise naturally. They are not something that family members decide through discussions or arguments. They all simply assume their roles without comment.

Theorem 3: Hierarchies Emerge Among the Roles

The roles that are needed in families, workplaces, or associations that share a specific space arise naturally, and they exist in two dimensions.

The first are **the roles that determine the direction of the family or group.** A specific group can thrive and grow in society or nature by determining its direction. In a family, that's the parents' role. In a company, that's the executives or managers.

One of the other functions of these roles **is to carry out specific**

movements in the direction that the top members of the group have determined. Just as a variety of jobs are necessary to maintain an organization, there are all kinds of unconscious roles in a family, and each member takes one of them on.

Some children assume a caretaking role in the family, while others make everyone laugh and create a lighthearted atmosphere. There are also many types of parents. There are those who exert their power over the children, and there are those who place importance on reasonable actions and talking things over. There are extremely affectionate mothers, and mothers who are even more unemotional and logical than the father of their families.

In that sense, families are divided into upper and lower ranks, but how this hierarchy plays out depends on the invisible relationships within each individual family.

For example, if the parents get divorced or one of the spouses becomes seriously ill or dies, there is no single, predictable result. In some cases, the remaining spouse remarries to fill the hole left by the absence of the deceased or departed spouse. In other cases, the remaining parent tries to fill both parental roles. There are even some families in which a child takes over the mother's role.

Theorem 4: Time Sequences Arise in the Space

In any space that humans are associated with, something meaningful is created. Families, in particular, create fixed spaces and human relationships that are handed down from parent to child, generation after generation.

Field theory gives us several points to consider when trying to understand a family's space. However, these theorems are not exactly what we can call "field theory." There is a flow of family legacies from generation to generation, and this is an attempt to apply field theory to this phenomenon.

This is where I will begin applying field theory to transgenerational issues. The way that Gestalt therapy looks at families is **in terms of how they are affected *here* and *now* by values, views of life, and attitudes, passed down through the generations**.

This gives rise to the need to take the time sequences that occur within the family into our consideration. Influences are passed from parent to child and from the child to the next generation in a time sequence. In order to preserve the family, the position of each member is determined silently. Once each person's position has been determined, their respective roles emerge from there, and for the family to exist in society, it must create a hierarchy of roles.

Then systems emerge that take on the job of transmitting those structures over time. In most cases, individuals are unaware of this, but these are the roles required since that individual was born; that individual's position within the family.

We might call these unspoken rules **agreements that family members make with one another to survive crises.**

4.3 The Development of Family Sculpture

So what is the theoretical background of these family sculptures that we have talked about earlier in the book?

One source is an outgrowth of **family therapy** developed by Virginia Satir (1916-1988). In the process of carrying out this therapy, she had third parties stand in a certain order like a sculpture, representing the members of the family by generation. The result was a representation of the relationships and communication patterns between parents and children.

It was only natural for Professor Hiroshi Inamura to incorporate family therapy into his treatment of children who refused to go to school, because he could see a visual representation of the relationship between the parents and the children. These visual representations gave him a true picture of the family's situation and made it easy to understand the relationships among the other members of the family.

The Development of the Genogram, a Psychological Family Tree

Murray Bowen (1913-1990) is thought of as the most prominent practitioner of family systems therapy, which he called "multigenerational theory." His **genograms**, or **psychological family trees**, have become part of the basic approach of family therapists today. They give us clear clues for understanding transgenerational phenomena when trying to solve family problems.

Family trees represent complex lineages and multiple generations, but genograms are used to help therapists understand the problems of families that have become dysfunctional. An example is found on the next page.

As family therapist John Bradshaw says in his 1996 book *Family Secrets: The Path from Shame to Healing*, "The genogram is a visual map of your family tree, but it includes more than your factual genealogy. It is used to gather information about family relationships over several generations It offers a broad frame of reference within which symptoms and problematic behavior can be understood in a new light."

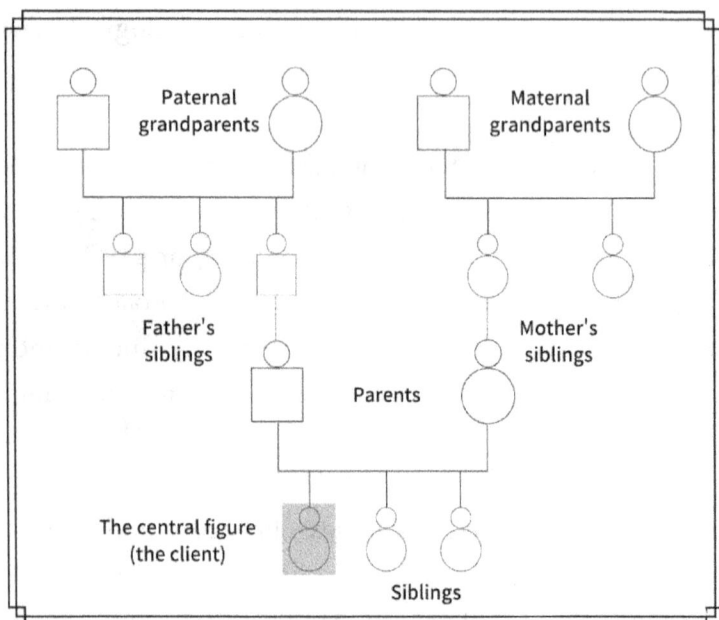

A Genogram (Psychological Family Tree)

Next to the symbol for each person, write the individual's full name, birthdate, level of education completed, date and cause of death, and physical and emotional problems. Inside the squares (which represent males) and the circles (which represent females), write the individual's current age. On the lines that connect married couples, such as parents and grandparents, write in the date of their marriage or divorce.

For example, suppose that creating the genogram reveals to the client that it was not his mother's side that had repeated problems with alcohol or sex addiction but his father's socially successful relatives. The client can discover these and other kinds of family secrets.

More recently, Bert Hellinger (1925-2019) extended this idea into what he called the **family constellation** and made it world-famous. Hellinger was born in Germany and entered a Catholic monastery at the age of twenty, after which he served as a Catholic priest for twenty-five years. Influenced by Africa's Zulu people, he began studying psychoanalysis in his late forties. Other major influences included primal therapy, Gestalt therapy, transactional analysis, and neurolinguistic programming (NLP).

The term "family constellation" was already in use in the field of family therapy. Hellinger studied family therapy and carried it over into his own work. Nowadays, if you mention family constellations, it is almost equivalent to mentioning his name, and the technique is highly regarded throughout the world.

With family constellations, Hellinger used the genogram technique to shed light on the dynamics of family systems that form the background of the illnesses, suffering, and violence the individual harbors. The technique thus disentangles the causes of these problems, the complications that he said are caused by love. I was deeply impressed by his observation that a family's problems are not due to someone being in the wrong but because the love that is within the family has become a tangled mess.

As I mentioned before, the theory laid out in this book is based on Gestalt therapy. If you would like to know more about it, I suggest reading my book *Kizuki no Serapii* (*Awareness Therapy*), which contains a fuller explanation. It includes a dialogue-based method called **the empty chair technique**. The client imagines sitting opposite an empty chair representing the person with whom he or she is in conflict and conducts a dialogue. Of course, the person imagined to be in the chair can be a parent or someone the client wants to understand.

In the empty chair technique, the client not only carries on dialogues with family members but also arranges the chairs that represent them. This technique thus makes the relationships among the members of the family visible.

Over the past twenty years or more, I have used the empty chair technique with more than 8,000 clients, and those experiences have brought intergenerational issues to my attention. I have chosen the term **family sculpture** as part of a theory of how intergenerational issues are represented in the empty chair technique and how to systematize this approach and make it easier to understand. I also like to distinguish family sculpture from Virginia Satir's family therapy or Hellinger's family constellations. In that sense, it is also an attempt to distinguish my technique from family sculpture as it is used in family therapy.

The Usefulness of the Empty Chair Technique

① Bringing the internal world to the surface

② Physical manifestation of the emotions

③ Making family conflicts (conflicted human relations) visible

④ Creating images of family impasses

⑤ Structures or patterns of intergenerational transmissions

⑥ Processing of the family's unsolved problems through improvisational drama

⑦ Completion of the Gestalt, or complete form, and integration of incomplete processes.

The Usefulness of the Empty Chair Technique

The family sculpture method, based on the empty chair technique, is a very useful means of understanding families. This technique takes a family's problems and **brings them to the surface, makes them visible, and creates an image of them,** allowing the therapist to **observe them objectively**. It can make the following factors clear and obvious.

By looking at the empty chairs arranged in front of them, not only the therapist but also the clients themselves—the people doing the emotional work—can see a clear picture of the family's unsolved problems. The emotions of the family members and the mutual stresses in their interpersonal relationships are brought to the surface. Awareness arises out of visualizing the conflicts among the members of the family.

When a family is at an impasse, bogged down in a problem, making the structural outline of the family's situation visible brings each individual's internal thoughts to the surface. Furthermore, individuals may express their emotions and moods in their bodies. These kinds of processes work to help us recover the entire shape, or Gestalt, of the family's situation.

As I mentioned before, the approach of revealing the invisible relationships among family members as they are **here** and **now** will also show us the relative positions of each member, expressed as vectors of **distance** and **direction**. These vectors allow us to observe the family as a dynamic group.

Some people are troubled by the relationships within their family. The empty chair technique allows them to see interpersonal relationships as living, dynamic energy, so that is why we have them arrange the chairs that represent the other family members in any position they choose.

The resulting **family sculpture** integrates the family sculpture used in family therapy with the empty chair technique of Gestalt therapy. In order to distinguish this new kind of family sculpture from the kind used in family therapy, I'll refer to it as a **family's sculpture**.

Let's take a look at the case of two young women whom I will call "A" and "B."

Both A and B are troubled by the interpersonal relationships in their families. Each one has trouble getting along with her mother. Both expressed their problems in similar ways: "I don't get along with my mother, and it's stressing me out."

In order to see A's and B's family sculptures, I had them create arrangements that showed the relationships among the members of their families.

A's Family

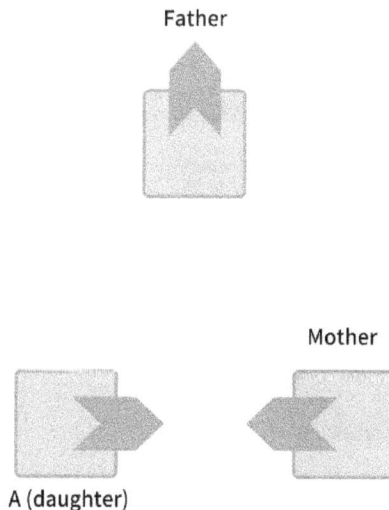

Note that even though both A and B say that they are troubled and stressed out by their relationships with their mothers, they have placed them in very different positions.

A may be expressing the fact that her father and mother do not get along, or the way that her mother expects her to be the one to hold the family together. A may be troubled because she cannot meet her mother's expectations. Her mention of feeling stress in dealing with her mother may be an expression of the fact that the family as a whole is not cohesive and everyone is tacitly expecting her to be the one who holds everything together.

B's family sculpture may be an indication that her father is unable to communicate with the rest of the family. On the other hand, it may mean that B is trying to do something about the conflict between her mother and father but can't make her father pay attention to her mother.

These family sculptures **do not have the same pattern**. If A and B were to express their feelings solely in words, they would say similar things, such as "I'm having trouble getting along with my family," or "I'm in conflict with them," or "I want us to understand one another," but the actual situations in their families are totally different.

Individual family members find their own "seats" within the family space, and it is possible to represent these positions in terms of distance and direction.

Distance represents **the depth and closeness of interpersonal relationships**, while **direction** represents **intimacy and conflict**, and both these factors can be represented by the concept of vectors.

In the field of physics, vectors are physical quantities that represent direction and size, and they are generally used when representing direction, intention, point of view, or coordinate axes. I have been viewing direction and intention with distance as one coordinate axis, and I treat the second coordinate axis as direction representing physical dynamics.

Theorem 1: Stress in the Family Manifests Itself as Distance

At the beginning, I have the client represent the relationships among family members in terms of distance. These distance vectors clearly identify the family's relationships and stresses.

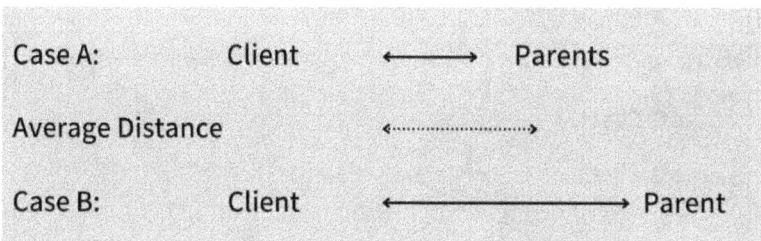

Case A:	Client	←——→	Parents
Average Distance		←·············→	
Case B:	Client	←————————→	Parent

In Case A, the distance among family members is short, so ties are formed through emotional connections such as love, hatred, or conflict. At times, family members are too close, so that their mutual desires and demands intensify. In such cases, a fundamental point of my approach is to find comfortable distances for everyone.

In Case B, the problem may be that relationships within the family are too distant. We can see that the love and other emotional ties between parents and children may be in conflict, may be alienated, or may be one-sided.

Theorem 2: Family Relationships Manifest Themselves as Direction

In forming the second vector, I have clients represent interpersonal relationships in their families in terms of direction. Adding direction allows visual observation of the psychological ties that make up the family. (See the chart below.)

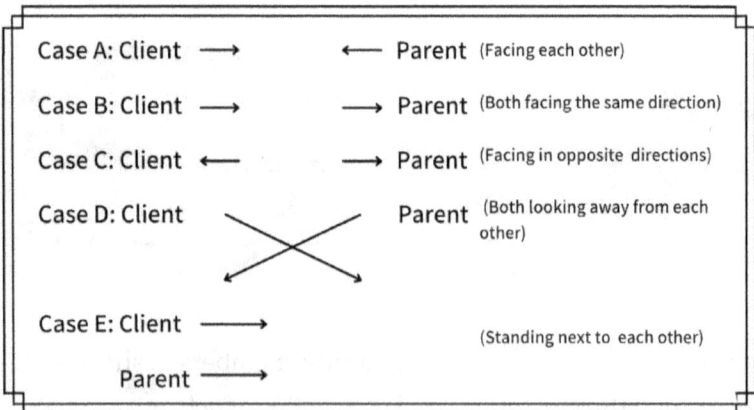

Case A: Client ⟶ ⟵ Parent	(Facing each other)
Case B: Client ⟶ ⟶ Parent	(Both facing the same direction)
Case C: Client ⟵ ⟶ Parent	(Facing in opposite directions)
Case D: Client ⤫ Parent	(Both looking away from each other)
Case E: Client ⟶ Parent ⟶	(Standing next to each other)

On the other hand, it may be that the client is begging his/her mother or father, "I want you to look at me."

In Case B, both the parent and the child are facing the same direction. The child may be hoping to follow in the parent's footsteps, or perhaps the parent has no interest in the child. When a parent looks away from the child, the child feels lonely and may interpret this attitude as meaning, "I intend to abandon you."

In Case C, both the parent and the child are facing in opposite directions. If that connotes an independent attitude, that's fine, but it may also indicate that the relationship is stressful.

In Case D, both the parent and the child are looking away from each other. In some cases, this means that their interest is focused on some other members of the family. In other cases, it means that one of them is looking away from the other to minimize stress.

In Case E, the parent and child are sitting next to each other and facing the same direction. This represents an especially close relationship between the parent and child.

Gestalt therapists are careful not to view family relationships in stereotyped ways, to avoid snap judgments such as "They're close together, so the relationship is good," or "They're far apart, so there are problems," or "They're facing away from each other, so there is conflict." Applying standard patterns to family situations seems to bring out the counselor's or therapist's preconceived notions.

These two vectors of distance and direction present us with clues for understanding a family, **but it is important to think of them as just a first step.**

The third vector necessary for understanding a family is determined according to the relative strength of the first vector (distance) and the second vector (direction). If Vector 1 is stronger, then it will pull Vector 3 toward itself. If Vector 2 is stronger, then Vector 3 will be pulled toward it. The relative positions of family members are therefore determined by the influences they receive from Vector 1 and Vector 2. They fall into place instantly, as determined by the magnetic field in the space, without anyone being aware of it.

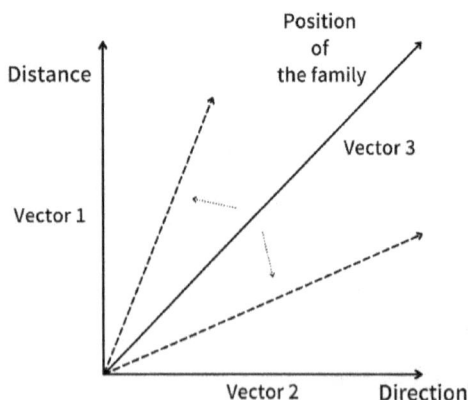

4.4 Unresolved Problems

In order to help you understand transgenerational issues, I'd like to discuss the concept of **unfinished business**, a basic concept of Gestalt therapy. In Japanese, we might talk about "unfinished matters" or "unresolved problems."

Fritz Perls understood human beings as organic entities. In his view, humans and animals are equipped with the ability to be aware of what they need to stay alive in the here and now.

For example, when they are dehydrated, they notice they're thirsty. When they need food, they feel hungry. When humans or animals are injured, they find a safe place to rest until their injury is healed. These are just a couple of ways in which living things function as organisms, feeling and noticing what they need to live.

This principle also applies to psychological matters. Humans have evolved into the most emotionally developed creature of all, and for that reason, they have already acquired the capacity to deal with unresolved emotional problems and the ability to seek ways of meeting unmet needs.

When human babies and children feel lonely or unloved, they seek out their mothers. When they feel anxious, they approach their mother and cling to her until they feel calm. This ability is at work even in adults. When adults want someone to lean on or when they feel lonely, they might phone a friend or get together with their family.

According to the same principle, human beings as living organisms have acquired the ability to be aware of what they need to fill the unresolved gaps in their emotional lives.

So what happens if people are unable to meet their vital needs? Their desire to solve that unresolved matter only increases. To take a physiological example, if people are thirsty and can't get their hands on water, their thirst increases. If they suppress their feelings of hunger, those feelings grow stronger. The principle here is that signs of physical needs only intensify if they are not met.

It's fair to say that emotional functions are the same. What happens if someone has a sad experience and suppresses his or her tears? What happens inside a lonely person who suppresses the desire to go mingle with other people? What happens inside an angry person who cannot express that anger?

In all these cases, the sorrow, the desire to get help from someone else, the loneliness, and the anger simply increase. That is, when emotions and feelings remain unexpressed, encountering the events or persons that caused the emotion provokes an overreaction.

In that way, unresolved feelings and experiences have an effect beyond time and space, and until they are resolved, they will resurface whenever a person encounters everyday stimuli.

These unfinished situations are called "unresolved problems." They can rise to the surface at any given point in the here and now as the person in question seeks a solution.

They carry with them unfinished emotions. These are feelings we are unaware of because we have suppressed them, and in our everyday lives their origins in these unresolved problems remain largely hidden from our consciousness.

Thus, here and now, at the present moment, it seems as if they do not exist, but in fact, they continue to exist within us. The concept of unresolved problems in Gestalt therapy refers to these problems that continue to exist, regardless of time or space.

So what happens if these unresolved problems involve more serious matters or experiences of violence? If people have had difficult experiences that they cannot talk about, they end up putting a lot of effort into repressing them and preventing them from coming to the surface of their consciousness. If these efforts at repression are too successful, people may act as if they have no unresolved problems at all.

The condition of being unable to find a solution for your problems and being unable to express them is called an

impasse. According to Professor Paula Bottom, mentioned in a previous chapter, Franz Perls borrowed a term from the Chinese author Lu Xun and referred to emotions that were at an impasse as "frozen fire." In other words, when you are at an impasse, it is as if your feelings appear to be frozen, but underneath it all, your emotions are smoldering.

Theorem 1: Unfinished Emotions and Experiences Exist Regardless of Time or Place

Unfinished emotions and experiences continue until they are brought to an end.

This can explain the circumstances of someone who claims to be "afraid" to interact with other people, who says, "I feel uncomfortable in groups or in spaces where people gather."

Such people often reveal during therapy sessions that they were bullied as a child or that their parents were physically abusive. In such situations, they were unable to express their feelings or freely express their anger at their tormentors.

When they encounter situations that remind them of those earlier experiences, their unfinished emotions and feelings rise to the surface. If the supervisor in their workplace reminds them of their parents, their unexpressed anger at their parents will be aroused.

One of my clients was brought up by parents who both had jobs and were too busy to pay much attention to him. Even as an adult, he felt lonely whenever he was by himself. In order to avoid that feeling, he kept looking for a girlfriend who would never leave him, one he could cling to and keep with him at all times.

This is how unfinished emotions and experiences continue to exist in people's minds, regardless of time or place. If people are aware of these emotions and experiences, they can fully experience them and bring them to an end by expressing them physically by a safe and nonthreatening method.

Theorem 2: Unresolved Problems Are Transmitted to the Next Generation

Matters that are more significant than unfinished emotions or experiences and painful events from the past are referred to as unresolved problems. Examples are being bullied at school as a child, being raised by parents who were always fighting, or growing up in an unloving household.

However, the parents responsible for these negative situations are often harboring their own unresolved problems. A father who is physically abusive toward his child may have been physically abused by his own mother and father. In turn, the child's grandparents may have grown up in economic circumstances that were so difficult that the family was broken up or there was a constant undercurrent of anxiety in the household. Many other kinds of negative circumstances can echo through the generations. If the child is extremely anxious, it may be because his or her parents are emotionally unstable. There are even some cases in which the child's grandparents were prone to emotional outbursts and were given to acting self-righteously within the family.

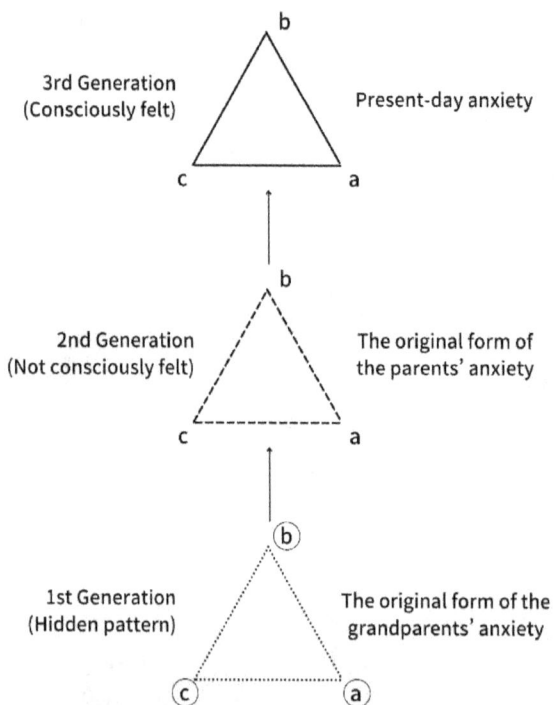

3rd Generation
(Consciously felt)

Present-day anxiety

2nd Generation
(Not consciously felt)

The original form of
the parents' anxiety

1st Generation
(Hidden pattern)

The original form of the
grandparents' anxiety

One woman with a three-generation problem complained of strong feelings of frustration and anxiety. However, the one who was truly in an unstable situation was her mother, since her father beat her when he was angry. However, counseling sessions revealed that the woman's grandfather had beaten his son (the woman's father) whenever anything went wrong, and the woman's grandmother had also been subject to his abuse. Witnessing these situations, the woman's father became subject to panic attacks.

In this case, my client's pattern of feeling anxiety and panic in the here and now was due not to her own unresolved problems but the conflict between her parents that occurred when she was a small child. In turn, the original form of her father's unresolved problems lay in the unresolved problems of his own parents' generation. As the figure with the three triangles shows, the unresolved problems of the first generation are represented by the dotted triangle at the bottom. The pattern established there is then transmitted to the next generation, and finally, to my client in the third generation.

Theorem 3: The Patterns of Unresolved Problems Are Repeated from Generation to Generation

Here's another example from a session I conducted in Australia. The client was herself a counselor, and after my group session was ended, she asked for an individual session. "I'm upset about my relationship with my daughter," she said. No matter how much I worry about her, she just scoffs and turns her back."

Her daughter was married and had two children, and she lived nearby, but whenever the two of them disagreed about the slightest thing, the daughter would say, "You're always on my back," and then make a big show of cuddling her own children. My client found this hurtful and began crying as she told me about it.

I had her arrange chairs to represent three generations. The first chair represented my client's daughter, turning her back on her mother. The second chair represented my client, turning her back on her own mother. Seeing this pattern, she experienced a flash of insight.

Her daughter's attitude of turning her back was the same attitude she had shown toward her own mother. In fact, she had "turned her back" to the extent of moving out of the house when she was twenty years old.

My client's mother was divorced and quite a worrywart, always interfering so much that my client could not stand it and left home at a young age, getting married in order to survive. Then she, too, was divorced, and she was able to keep her daughter close at hand over the years. However, her daughter's hurtful habit of turning her back was exactly what my client had done to her own mother. No doubt my client's mother also felt hurt when this happened, and now her daughter was repeating the behavior.

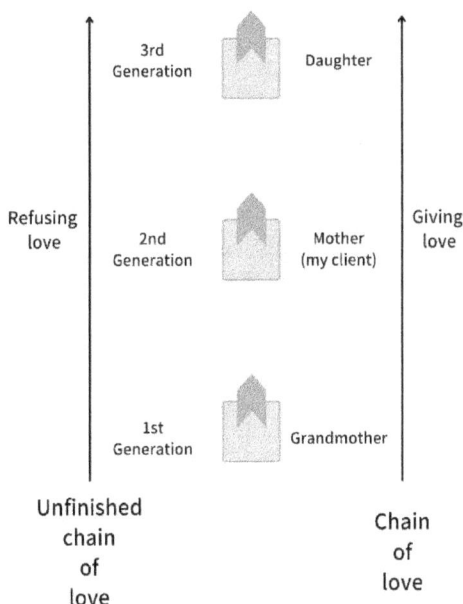

In some cases, showering a child with love can lead to conflict. As in this case, when a divorced mother and her daughter are unable to express their love for each other, a family a transgenerational negative legacy of love arises.

Theorem 4: A Family's Unresolved Problems Are Expressed as Family Impasses

When a family member is harboring unresolved problems, it is expressed as an impasse. For example, suppose a father takes out his individual emotions on his family. If the members of the family are unable to resist his violence or domineering attitude,

Masatsugu Momotake

then his problems make everyone suffer. Impasses like this can continue for years.

A mother who never received enough expressions of love from her own mother may be unable to express enough love for her own daughter. The daughter feels unloved and alone and becomes angry with her mother, feelings that can manifest themselves as conflict. Or take the example of a child who is bullied and refuses to attend school. This issue makes the entire family suffer, and they may up in an impasse in which they cannot find a way to solve the problem.

It can also happen that a member of the family dies suddenly due to unforeseen circumstances. Everyone in the family experiences sorrow at the passing of their loved one, but they may try to avoid these feelings by not mentioning the incident.

At such times, if the family members tread carefully around one another's unfinished emotions, a rigid impasse is reached and continues. They send one another tacit messages about now talking about their shared grief, but ironically, that turns their grief into a "frozen fire" that never goes away. These patterns of not mentioning worries and sorrows and the psychological structures that the family creates are passed down to the next generation as a "negative legacy of love."

Theorem 5: Negative Legacies of Love Are Transmitted as Conflict Until People Are Aware of Them

We need to classify families' problems as those due to an individual member's unresolved problems and those due to impasses manifested as conflicts created by the family's system. The reason is that the latter kinds of problems do not belong solely to the individuals who are suffering from them. Impasses created by the family's system, these kinds of unresolved problems, are not individual problems.

Similarly, even if a family's problems seem to be the problems of the family as it is now, they may be intergenerational problems handed down like a legacy—and if so, new processes arise when the current family becomes aware of the fact. What lies behind most familial conflict is not just "family problems" but a lack of love intertwined with an intergenerational legacy.

By exposing these patterns, structures, and systems to the light of day, families can choose between characteristics that they need to inherit and characteristics that they do not need to inherit. We can focus people's attention on their family's hidden messages and make them aware that these messages exist. When family members are aware of these messages, then they can choose which ones to pay attention to.

4.5 Systems of Somatic Memory

4.5.1 What is Somatic Memory?

Somatic memory refers to the way people remember experiences in their bodies. In current educational theory, we are taught that memory is a function of the brain, so the concept of somatic memory may seem strange to people who hold that belief. Some people even take it to be an unscientific notion.

Yet recent research into physiology and neurology has yielded a lot of data that supports the existence of somatic memory. Many scientists have started to turn their attention to bodily phenomena. This is why researchers in Europe and North America have begun taking up the field of **somatic psychology**. Until recently, psychological and psychiatric therapy on the one hand and bodywork on the other have been considered completely separate fields, but now somatic psychology has become a central concern within them and has begun to exert a major influence on them.

In simple terms, somatic psychology is a therapeutic trend that integrates the body and the mind. For example, Takashi Kubo gives the following extremely interesting exposition:

In 1985, the American neurobiologist Candace Pert found that neuropeptides exist in the cell walls of both the brain and the immune system. That means that neuropeptides, neurotransmitters, and other endocrine substances have a direct effect on the immune system, so that there are close connections between the emotions and immunology. Emotions are not created only in the brain but in all the cells of the entire body. That is, our entire bodies are literally an unconscious seat of emotions. Our emotions (whether positive or negative) are produced chemically on the cellular level where they accumulate.

Wilhelm Reich (1897-1957) is considered the father of somatic psychology. He is best known in psychological and psychotherapy circles in Japan for introducing the concept of **character armor**, which leads to the further concept of **muscular armor**. In simple terms, psychological character armor becomes bodily muscular armor.

Reich's view of the unity of mind and body underlies the basic theories of Gestalt therapy. He was the first psychoanalyst to say, "Emotions are lodged in the muscles."

So how are those things that we call "memories" remembered? According to Reich, they are remembered in both the muscles and the emotions.

Franz Perls, the creator of Gestalt therapy, said, "We say that we have bodies, but that is a major problem." In other words, we think that our individual selves are the essential entities, more so than our bodies. It's a belief that our bodies are something outside of ourselves, and that the individual self is in charge, while the body is disparaged as subordinate to the self.

Perls says this is not true, that the body is the individual self. We can have a sense of ourselves as individuals thanks to our bodily senses. We feel sadness as something inside our chest, and it is because of this physical sensation that we realize we are sad. Since muscle tension in the back or the head is felt as a physical sensation, we realize that we are in pain. We can feel when our stomach is empty, so we realize we are hungry.

If we can take this approach, our bodies loom large in making sense of our experiences.

Theorem 1: Memory Stems from Links Between Our Bodies, Our Sensations, and Our Brains

I'd like to return to the concept of somatic memory, the idea that "the body is the home of my life memories." If we take this view, we can understand the significance of the body in two ways.

One of these is to think of the body as something that carries our life's experiences as it lives from moment to moment and from hour to hour. When you are taking a walk, you notice that your body is walking. But why is this the case?

When you put your right foot forward, you feel the movement of your blood and muscles. At the same time, your internal sense of balance, your grasp of your body's position in space, and the feeling of your foot making contact with the surface beneath you are sent to your brain as signals. When you eat, you experience the food through your sense of taste. A few minutes after that, the vibrations from chewing your food are transmitted to the brain, and acid is secreted to put the digestive juices into action. When your stomach starts digesting the food, your brain senses its internal movements, and the muscles in your intestines prepare to move in peristaltic waves. When you watch a comedy on TV and start laughing, you experience that laughter as movements of your facial muscles and lips. If you are watching a tragic drama, the plot developments arouse feelings of sadness in you, which you feel in the form of tightness in your chest.

The second way we can understand the significance of the body is to realize that the brain—which is, after all, a part of our body—perceives your body's experiences, and not only in terms of emotions, such as sadness. As you become aware of a pain in your finger, you see blood oozing out of it and you think, "I've cut my finger." It is also possible for you to realize that you are angry. All in all, your body's sensations tell you what has happened and what you are aware of. You can understand the meaning of what you feel based on past experiences and knowledge.

That is due to the development of our brains, which find the meanings of our experiences and classify them by comparing them with previous experiences. Animals, too, act based on their bodily senses, but many of these actions are instinctive, and the animal is not aware of its own actions. Humans are the only creatures who are aware that they have awareness. Humans are the only creatures who are aware of their own actions, assign meaning to them, and acknowledge them.

Dr. Gordon Wheeler of the Esalen Institute in California came to Japan on the occasion of the establishment of the Japan Gestalt Therapy Association, and on that occasion, he spoke about the relationship between Gestalt theory and the brain. The things that people are aware of via their brains are called "experiences," "lived experiences," or "memories." However, recent brain research has revealed that the part that recognizes the body's experiences is the so-called "new brain," the cerebral neocortex. The stimuli that people receive from the outside world are transmitted to the brain by the nerves, but the neocortex does not receive sensory stimuli directly. Various parts within the brain take in the sensory information, and it is the neocortex that recognizes its meaning. For that reason, people can receive the same stimulus and experience it differently, and people who have experienced the same event may remember them as different bodily experiences. This is the view of Gestalt therapy, which understands humans to be very creative.

Memory consists of somatic memory and mental memory working in concert. Furthermore, memories can be intensified by emotions, since there is a system that causes the entire organism to remember strong feelings and emotions. These emotions serve to tie somatic memories and mental memories together, and memories come into being when three elements are linked: bodily sensations, such as those in the muscles; the neocortex, which recognizes and assigns meaning to these sensations; and the emotions that well up within the body. In that sense, memories are the result of a three-part association between the body, emotions, and the brain.

Theorem 2: The Body is Where Our Life Memories Are Lodged

People notice when their own muscles are tense. If they turn their attention to this stress, they can become aware of the memory in which that stress is lodged. This is the result of a triangular relationship between their muscle memory, their emotions, and the brain, which perceives all of this.

A Personal Experience with the Body and Memory

The experience I am going to talk about took place in 2001 during a session with Dr. Ronald A. Alexander, a Gestalt therapist who had been trained in hypnosis by psychiatrist Milton H. Erickson and had learned body psychotherapy from

Alexander Lowen, a disciple of Reich. He had been studying somatic psychology since his youth.

I hoped to find out sometimes about my own body and memories. He abruptly focused on my right thigh and directed me to stretch my right thigh, kneel with my right knee on the tatami floor, and my left knee pulled in toward my body. This posture stretched my iliopsoas (hip flexor) muscle and the muscular layer of my large intestine. He then told me to start panting. After two or three minutes of panting, I felt the muscles in my right thigh and right hip flexors grow hot. Alexander urged me to continue panting while feeling that sensation of heat. After I while, the muscles in my right thigh began to feel unbearably stretched and painful. At that point, a scene from my childhood suddenly came to mind.

It happened when I was in third or fourth grade in elementary school, and it is something that I recall from time to time.

I was with some children from the neighborhood, acting out a superhero scenario, when I got carried away and head-butted another boy in the nose. He was older than me and always tried to act like a tough guy, so he flew into a rage and start punching my head.

I burst into tears and ran home. As I came into our yard, I saw my father working on an oil painting. I remember sobbing, "Dad!" as I came into the yard. My father didn't answer but kept painting while he waited for me to stop crying. When I had stopped crying, he turned and looked at me and said, "Go back and play with the other kids." I remember that I returned to the group of children after hearing those words. My memory of that situation exists alongside recollections of my father's calm demeanor as he pursued his favorite hobby of oil painting.

Then a memory from my high school years, from the time when my father took a new job in Akita, came to mind. One of his subordinates was a former sumo wrestler who raised Akita dogs. Along with the scene with my father painting in the yard, I recalled how my father acquired one of those dogs from him and brought it home.

It became my job to take that dog for a walk every day. Yet when my father developed cancer and came home from the hospital after undergoing surgery, the dog refused to come near him. He took the dog outside into the yard and looked at it tenderly. "The dog recognizes the odor of cancer," he said, without taking offense. About a year later, my father died. I was twenty years old at the time.

Those memories of my father intersected with memories of my own life. My father was quite a drinker, and he came home from work drunk every day. As I look back, I think that he may have been an alcoholic. When I was in junior high school, we moved to Fukuoka. While we were there, my father sometimes passed out on the street. I recall two occasions when the police at the local substation informed us, and my mother and I had to go bring him home.

Since we moved to Akita when I was in high school, we had to deal with heavy snowfalls. It was my job to stay awake studying and watch so that my father would not pass out between our front gate and the front steps when he came home. My slender mother would have been unable to rouse and move my father if he passed out in our front yard.

When my father, a company employee, died, our family lost its economic stability. We were living in company-owned housing in Akita, so we had to leave and rent a small rowhouse. After I somehow managed to obtain a university education, our family moved to Tokyo.

Even after I graduated from the university, I lived in a small apartment in Tokyo with my mother and my younger brother, who was still a student, while my youngest brother rented a room nearby. We simply did not have the kind of income that would have allowed us all to live together. Our mother began working as a nurse's aide in a hospital. In those days, patients had either family members or hired help to take care of their non-medical needs when they were hospitalized, so she would sleep on a mat by the patient's bed. Having had tuberculosis when she was younger, she could not do any kind of heavy work, so evidently, this was what she was able to find. Thinking of this, I was reminded of how much she suffered during her life.

In addition to these "lost experiences," I talked about how I was determined not to become a company employee like my father, and I also discussed the physical aspects of how I felt when our lives became more difficult after my father's death. Despite her frailty, my mother worked without ever complaining. I noticed that I felt myself to be a poor excuse for an oldest son since I didn't protect my mother.

As I spoke about these things, I noticed my chest muscles tightening and that the tension came from inside my chest. It felt as if some sort of clear liquid was slowly flowing from my chest inside my body and pooling near my stomach, and the tightness in my chest gradually moved into my stomach. At that point, I suddenly recalled a time during my childhood when I fell into the reservoir that I was accustomed to visiting when I had free time. I had caught a small fish, and when I tried to get it into my net, I lost my balance and fell into the water

Instead of being frightened, I felt myself slowly rotating as I sank into the water. After I had rotated a few times, my head suddenly bobbed up above the water. I was rescued when my brother and friends, who happened to be there, extended the net toward me and pulled me out.

As I spoke about this incident, I felt as if the muddy water I had swallowed in the reservoir lay stagnant in my stomach. Spasms in my stomach pushed this muddy water up into my throat. I gave an involuntary choked cry, and this muddy water came pouring out of my throat onto the floor.

Now that I'm an adult, I sometimes go to Musashi-Kosugi, a suburb of Tokyo, to see that reservoir. However, the area looks nothing like it did during my childhood. It's all built up with commercial buildings and condominiums.

I was really fond of that reservoir in the old days. The neighborhood children went to the reservoir and the nearby open field to play every day. We have lost that bit of nature, and there are no more places like it left in the Tokyo area. I wonder if the empty feeling I get when I consider this loss is what reminded me of my father. The loss of my father and the loss of the place where I played as a child have intersected in my somatic memory.

This session with Dr. Alexander taught me that my somatic memory has woven together a meaning for my life made up of enjoyable, happy moments and sad, bereft moments, memories of my father, and memories of my childhood.

Your body, first of all, assumes the burden of your life experiences. Everything you did as a child—crying, quarreling, being injured, laughing, eating—resides in your muscles.

Second, your brain, which is after all part of your body, has a cognitive mechanism context that shows you the meanings of your experiences. You grow up with experiences and feelings that create your worldview and that your body and brain remember: "I have decided not to become a company employee like my father" or "I hate the fact that I didn't protect my mother" or "It was so hard to lose my family" or "I enjoyed living close to nature."

If we view the connection between the mind and body in this way, we can see that the idea that your brain is the control center for everything is no longer tenable. Rather, it seems that your memories start with your body, move into your emotions, and are stored in your brain in a sort of chain reaction, and it is your brain that assigns meaning to them.

Theorem 3: Hidden Messages About the Family Are Transmitted to the Next Generation as Somatic Memories

Now we turn to transgenerational issues: how they might be connected to somatic memory, how the parents' values and views of life are transmitted to the children within the family system, and how the parents' incomplete decisions and unresolved problems are transmitted to the next generation, and in what form. How are your own individual views of life and somatic memories handed down to your children within the family system?

Of course, your views of life and your experiences can be transmitted within the family system through verbal communication, through what you talk about with your children. However, in the fields of psychology and psychotherapy, it is known that that messages expressed in somatic (bodily) terms have a stronger effect than messages transmitted through words.

4.5.2 The Significance of Mirror Neurons

In recent years, the discovery of mirror neurons has caused a stir. These mirror neurons are nerves within the brain that can imitate people's movements and expressions like a mirror. They were discovered in the early 1990s by Italian researchers Giacomo Rizzolatti, Leonardo Fogassi, and Vittorio Gallese.

These mirror neurons are at work when parents share their values and worldviews through their bodies. To paraphrase one simple explanation found in Takashima (2006), people's mirror neurons are not merely nerve cells that imitate simple movements but neurons that reproduce movements and expressions inside the onlooker's mind and read the other person's moods and thoughts.

In other words, thanks to these mirror neurons, you can sense other people's moods and circumstances with your body. This means that children learn to understand the meanings of emotions, gestures, and actions by seeing (and unconsciously imitating) their parents' actions, postures, and movements. To put it more clearly, they learn the meanings of what their parents transmit to them with their bodies.

For example, parents can send all kinds of messages about their worldview to their children without using words: "My life is sad," or "Life is a battle," or "Don't trust other people."

Children thus receive physical messages about what their parents are feeling without the parents being aware they are sending these messages. Because their mirror neurons imitate their parents, children have a physical experience of their parents' emotions and attitudes.

For that reason, the unconscious, nonverbal messages that parents (either mothers or fathers) transmit to their children penetrate deeply. Then, when the children become adults, they, in turn, transmit physical messages to the next generation.

Since all members of the family have mirror neurons in their brains, the parents, too, can sense their children's emotions from their postures, actions, and expressions, even without communicating verbally. Of course, they can share the children's happiness, and an entire family can share sorrow or anger.

The Third Factor

I have already shown that in a family sculpture, two of the factors in determining the position of a person's chair are the vectors of **distance** and **direction**, but the third factor is the body, or more precisely, its **posture**. Adding this third factor allows us to understand the family's unresolved problems.

If memories are made up of links between the body, brain, and emotions, then memory is a three-dimensional phenomenon. In other words, unfinished business and unresolved problems exist in space as three-dimensional entities.

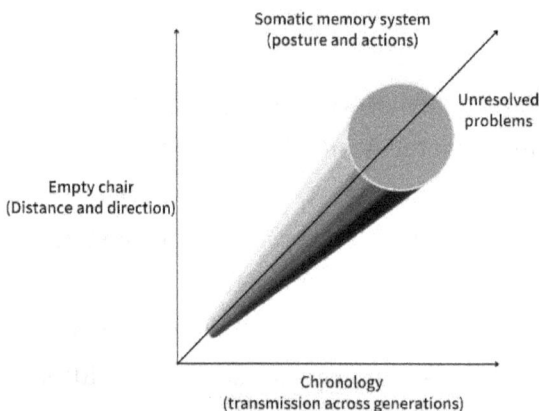

Somatic memory system
(posture and actions)

Unresolved
problems

Empty chair
(Distance and direction)

Chronology
(transmission across generations)

(1) Represent the relations among family members in terms of distance and direction using the Empty Chair technique (family sculpture)

(2) Add time and generation to the space

(3) See postures and bodies transmitted by somatic memory

Transgenerational issues, including unfinished business and unresolved problems, continue in a chain across generations, but these three factors can bring them to the surface in the **here** and **now**. It is through working with these three factors that we can begin to approach and understand our own transgenerational issues.

Inheriting the Worldviews of One's Parents

As I thought about mirror neurons and somatic memory, I recalled a scene that took place when my daughter was four or five years old. One morning, I was leaving the house a bit earlier than usual. I was wearing a suit and walking quietly toward the front door so as not to wake the family in the room that we all shared.

I heard my daughter say, "Daddy, are you going to play golf *again?*"

Hearing her voice, I froze in place. Even though she had spoken softly and slowly, she sounded just like my mother, with undertones of the voice my wife used when scolding me about wasting money. I turned at the sound of the uncannily familiar voice to see my daughter watching me from her futon.

"How did she know?" I whispered to myself, my heart pounding. My daughter didn't even know what golf was. I played only about once a month when I had a little extra pocket money, but I pretended that I was going to work so that my family wouldn't know.

Even so, how did she know? I was really flustered. Her "*again?*" sounded louder to me than it really was.

She may have guessed what was going on because I acted differently than usual. Maybe it was because I was sneaking out, suppressing my delight at the prospect of playing golf, and walking hunched over. Whatever the case may be, my daughter had seen me and learned that this situation was one in which her mother tended to say critically, "Golf *again?*"

My wife had not taught this to our daughter intentionally. Instead, our daughter had seen such exchanges between us and learned that "When Dad walks like that, it's something to be harshly criticized," thus copying my wife's values. Because she had mirror neurons, she had acquired the rules and practices of our family structure. At the age of four or five, she had internalized her mother's values, and, in fact, both our daughter and our son gradually took on their parents' values and worldview.

Family sculptures based on distance and direction make it relatively easy to understand patterns of family behavior. Adding somatic memory to the mix highlights current family impasses, and in some cases, even unfinished business from previous generations emerges. The following two case studies are examples of this.

Case 13: A Family's Shared Grief

Toshio Yamanaka was a businessman in his forties. At one point, he was unable to go to work for nearly a year due to severe depression. He recovered and returned to work, but after six months, his depression returned. That was when he decided to go for counseling and participated in one of my sessions.

He was married but had no children, so when it came time for him to create his family sculpture, I had him represent his family of origin. He arranged his parents, himself, and his older sister in something like a circle—not really a circle, but a space with rounded corners.

I had him choose people from the group to represent the members of his family and told him to assign each of them a posture. I then told each of these people to feel the physical sensations that these postures aroused.

After a while, the woman portraying Toshio's mother said that she felt grief. The man portraying his father said, "I'm too choked up to speak." The people portraying his sister and himself were staring into the middle of the rounded space. They knelt with their hands on the floor as if to avoid being absorbed into the space.

After the session, Toshio talked to his parents and older sister. It was in this conversation that he learned about the family's firstborn son. He knew that he had an older brother who had died in childhood, but his parents had never told him the details.

The family had gone to visit his father's parents, who lived in an old-style farmhouse. While they were there, the boy fell into the open hearth on the main floor and suffered severe burns, which eventually killed him. All this had happened before Toshio was born.

Evidently, no one in the family ever talked about this tragic occurrence. Even so, his mother's grief was transmitted to everyone. His father blamed himself and was obsessed with thoughts of, "If only I hadn't taken him to visit my parents," but he never expressed these thoughts out loud. However, Toshio's mother and sister could feel his thoughts as a physical sensation.

Despite not talking about the tragedy, the family shared their grief with one another physically through postures, facial expressions, and tone of voice. This is how Toshio came to share the family's sad experience at an early age.

It may be that unconsciously, he felt it would be wrong for him to succeed at work or as a member of society. He may have been punishing himself for being unable to serve as a satisfactory replacement for his older brother. In any case, it seems that shedding light on the family's hidden messages allowed him to start moving forward.

Thus, bringing impasses into conscious awareness instills new energy in a family.

The second case study is about transgenerational issues and a chain of somatic memories. Sometimes, people are unaware of things that ought to be clear, creating a hidden dynamic within a family.

Case 14: A Hidden Dynamic

Moriyuki Ichijo suffered from stiff shoulders and migraines, and he came to me to talk about his symptoms because he suspected they were connected to family issues, specifically with relations between himself and his son, who was the presumed heir to the family business.

After graduating from the university, the son had gone to work, but he said that he did not feel like inheriting the family business. Instead, he changed jobs, was transferred to the U.S., and showed no sign of coming back.

"I have two daughters," Moriyuki said, "but we have a tradition of letting only males take charge of the business."

In order to visualize relations within the family, I had him create a family sculpture. What became obvious immediately was that the son had literally turned his back on the family. Moriyuki and his wife were sitting side by side, facing the same direction, but their son was sitting in front of them, also facing the same direction instead of looking at them.

Looking at the representation of the son, I got an impression of impatience and irritation. I asked Moriyuki how old his son was. "Thirty," he grumbled. "In the old days, he would have already taken over the business."

Since Moriyuki was obviously concerned about who would inherit the business, I asked him how long the business had been in the family. "Nineteen generations," he immediately replied.

I then had him choose people to represent those nineteen generations of ancestors. I had the people who represented the five generations immediately before his play a role. I had the rest of the generations simply stand in the back.

Moriyuki then told the people who represented the various generations what posture they should assume. He asked the person who represented the founder of the business to stand in a rigid posture, but from there on down the generations, there were occasionally people who strayed away from the direct line.

The most recent was Moriyuki's grandmother, who had rebuilt the Ichijo family fortunes. The generation before that included people who had left the line or who were sitting down and not moving.

I then asked each person to state their message to the following generations in one phrase. For example, the person portraying Moriyuki might say to his son, "I'm annoyed with you," or "Grow up and take over the business."

The grandmother who had married into the family and then rebuilt the business stood straight and tall and said, "I will never give up." Her husband stood aside from the main line and leaned on her, saying, "I'm depending on you."

Of course, the people who were portraying the ancestors from previous generations had never seen nor met one another. Yet the people in every generation who had rebuilt the business or increased its prosperity were people who had been talked about. From this demonstration, it became clear that the family regarded those ancestors who had built up or rebuilt the business to be "fine people," while regarding the others as "failures."

I told the people portraying the ancestors to say something together all at once. The participants from the generations that were regarded as "fine people" shouted, "Stick with it!" and "We're depending on you!" while those who had been belittled mumbled, "I'll try" or "Well . . ." With participants portraying nineteen generations all shouting or mumbling at once, the room echoed with a sound like that of Buddhist monks chanting the sutras or repeating the *nenbutsu*, the prayer to Amida Buddha.

As Moriyuki listened to that chant-like sound, his shoulders stiffened and he felt a migraine coming on. He suddenly said, "I have not been doing anything to make the Ichijo family business prosper." It may be that he unconsciously identified with the ancestors who were considered failures in the family's traditional lore. He then told each generation of ancestors in turn that he had no intention of going out of business. As he did so, the chant-like voices gradually quieted down, including the ones that had been shouting, "Stick with it!"

I am looking forward to finding out what effect this experience will have on Moriyuki's relationship with his son. No matter what, there exist chains of somatic memories that are handed down through the generations, almost like "emotional genes." Just like DNA, these life experiences appear to be passed along to the next generation.

Conclusion: Looking Closely at Your Ancestors

5.1 An Occurrence at a Street Stall

One Friday evening, I was having a beer, sitting at the counter of one of the street stalls that the city of Fukuoka is famous for, a stall that the front desk clerk at my hotel had recommended as offering particularly delicious food. I found that the cool evening temperatures of early summer enhanced my enjoyment of the beer, and once I had finished it off, I ordered a bowl of the seafood stew known as *o-den*.

In the seats behind me were four or five middle management types in their twenties or thirties who were already drunk.

I heard one of the young men say in the local dialect, "So you see . . ." and "What I mean to say is . . ."

He seemed to be trying to convey the opinions of the rank-and-file workers to a colleague.

The colleague shouted angrily, "If you worry about things like that, the company will never grow!"

The discussion was becoming heated. Being a bit drunk myself,

I watched the proceedings with some interest.

The owner of the stall also appeared to be listening to the exchange between the two young men. His attitude toward them was something you would expect. He neither overreacted to the two drunk customers nor acted indifferent to them. He had some freedom to act. I thought to myself, "He knows how to handle things."

Then suddenly, the colleague roared, "You bastard! Are you saying it was wrong to put me in charge?" He rose up as if encouraged by his own loud voice and grabbed the first man by the hair.

There was a young couple who helped out at the stall, and the husband rushed out to try to break up the fight.

"Oh, don't stop them," I whispered to myself. "They're just getting started."

The elderly owner's wife came out, and with a broad grin, she poured me a glass of *shochu* liquor. I admired her ability to handle things.

The young couple who worked at the stand stood around and watched, but when the husband tried to stop the fight, his intervention seemed only to make the confrontation more intense.

Bash! came the sound of someone being hit on the face or head.

Instead of getting angry, the young man who had been hit extended his hand to his staggering drunk colleague and let him lean on his shoulder. Then, with a simple, "We're leaving," the group headed off toward the station.

I was impressed by the scene I had just witnessed. "Young people in Fukuoka sure are hot-tempered!" I thought.

Even so, I was impressed by what you might call the relaxed and generous attitude of the elderly couple who ran the street stall. They left their customers free to behave any way they wanted.

"This evening was a great way to end the day," I thought as I staggered back to my hotel. Ever since then, I occasionally recalled the incident at the street stall. It taught me something significant about human beings.

Precisely because individuals unconsciously play out certain roles, they can assume positions that are appropriate for these roles.

The Leader (The Elderly Man Who Managed the Street Stall)

This man cooks ramen and *o-den* without saying a word. He is not indifferent to the young men's argument, but he does not take any action. The leader's role is to keep the site safe. He quietly keeps watch to make sure that the people around him and those who are uninvolved in the dispute are not affected by the young men's quarrel.

This is the role expected of high-level managers in companies and workplaces. Social or economic problems with the company's customers or suppliers may arise, but personnel who can handle these situations without taking any action are those who serve as leaders.

In a family, this is the father's role, or at least the man's role. If there are problems with the children or if they start quarreling, he never gets involved in picking the situation apart. He keeps an eye on things to determine whether this is a problem that they can solve by themselves.

The Leader's Supporter (The Elderly Woman at the Street Stall)

The old woman grins as she watches the young men quarrel. She has ascertained that the situation does not require any action on the part of the other customers and indicates that with her casual, cheerful attitude.

At the same time, she helps maintain the business by pouring beer and *shochu* so that the customers don't get up and leave.

She projects an image of believing that it's alright for young people to behave that way.

In Japanese society, older people are expected to play that role. In a family, it is the mother who plays that role. When someone in the family is in poor health or under a lot of stress, she tells the rest of the family to have consideration for that person.

The Rescuer (The Young Husband)

Whenever trouble occurs, the Rescuer immediately tries to bring the situation under control. Whenever trouble or conflict arises, he moves to solve the problem. Because he acts quickly. The people around him receive the message that some sort of emergency has arisen. As a result, he stirs up feelings of stress and anxiety in the group.

In a family situation, it is meddlesome neighbors who play this role. In a preschool or school, groups of teachers play this role.

The Focus of Attention (The Two Young Men)

They exhibit the most energy of the people in this setting. They try to work out a conflict as they drink. One of them makes arguments and offers opinions about the welfare of the company as a whole, while the other resists him and plays the role of rebel.

In a family, the mother asks the father to do things for the family and to be more involved in the children's lives. In response, the father takes a contrary attitude and either says he is too busy with work or acts indifferent to whatever is happening at home.

When these kinds of structural roles evolve naturally within a family, each of the members not only gains a sense of satisfaction but also is open to connections with the larger society.

Time Sequence: From the Grandparents to the Young Couple and the Grandchildren

The members of the family that runs that street stall in Fukuoka are probably satisfied with what they are doing, and they are most likely proud of their responsibilities in playing out their various roles and respect one another's abilities. Of course, the grandfather, who is not very articulate, is unlikely to express such feelings in words, but we can assume that he is able to acknowledge his wife and the young couple in other ways. Similarly, the cheerful attitude of the young couple expresses their feelings.

The owner's grandchildren, who are in the early years of elementary school, also come out of the street stall. They eat ramen while watching what their parents do and absorbing memories of their grandparents that will remain with them forever.

* * *

A year later, I went back to the location of the street stall to see how it was faring. However, it was no longer there. I wondered if something had happened to the family, or whether the grandfather had fallen ill or the grandmother had died.

I stood there for a long time, asking myself these questions. I happened to glance down at my feet and saw a red brick soaked through with cooking oil, lying there as if it was meant to teach me a lesson.

I stared at the traces of oil on the brick for a while. I knew that this area was always kept clean and tidy, so I understood that these traces of oil were not of recent origin. They indicated that the owners of the stall had worked here for many years and raised their children here.

5.2 The Body Always Moves Toward Love

As I stood looking at the brick on the ground, I thought back to a scene from twenty years before, a scene from a town near Cape Erimo, located on the opposite end of Japan on the island of Hokkaido.

I had reached Cape Erimo by taking the Hidaka Railway Line out of Sapporo to the last station and continuing onward by bus. I had spent the previous night in a town along the Hidaka Line in a traditional inn, a *ryokan* made of wood, located across the street from the station and bearing a name that translates to "The Inn in Front of the Station."

I wandered lazily around the town for about two days, and on one of my walks, I entered the grounds of a Buddhist temple. Next to the garden was a path that led uphill, and I was following it when I noticed all the Buddhist statues along the way.

These statues, many of which appeared to represent the *bodhisattva* Jizo, were of all different shapes and sizes. However, when I looked back down the path from the concentration of statues, I could look out over the sea.

I don't know whether the statues were from the late nineteenth or early twentieth century, but they were old enough that the details of their faces had eroded away.

The variation in the faces and shapes of the statues indicated that they had most likely not been installed by a single specific group of people. It may have been the result of a village custom.

When a villager died, his or her family may have placed these images along the hillside path to watch over people who went out fishing. In fact, it is believed that the temple was built after the statues were set up.

We all watch over or keep our eyes on something. People journey to temples or shrines to offer prayers for the safety or happiness of their families. Alternatively, they may climb a small hill and think of their families back home as they look down on the houses below.

Even so, our mind's eye may be visualizing religious images. The scenes, events, and people that appear before our eyes evoke thoughts of distant family members and ancestors.

The religious images that we treasure in our hearts sometimes receive hidden messages of our families that we are unaware of.

Case 15: The Force That Attracts You

Kayoko Yokomine, a nurse, told me about some concerns she had.

"I don't have any particular problems with my family," she said, "but I want to understand what is going on between us. Recently, I've started dating a certain man.

"However, I have a sense that there's some sort of connection between him and my family. Yet the moment I saw him, I felt that our meeting was meant to be. Actually, he felt the same way. It feels as if we're connected by an invisible thread.

"Still, I'm confused. I don't think that I love this man. Despite that," she said, extending her left hand, "I felt as if something was grabbing my hand and pulling me in his direction.

"My mother keeps close watch on all of us in the family. We're the type of family in which the men aren't much of a presence at home and do whatever they want outside the home. My father spends his days off at pachinko parlors, and my older brother does whatever he feels like.

"My grandmother ran the household like a tight ship. She was widowed at a young age but managed the household and raised my father all by herself. My mother is the same type. In fact, my grandmother chose her as a wife for her son.

"I think that's why my mother lets my father and brother do whatever they please. I used to think that a woman's role in life was to make life easy for her husband and take care of the household."

At that point, I asked Kayoko to create a family sculpture. As she positioned the people representing her family around the room, I noticed that, as expected, she placed her mother at the center.

She placed herself in front of her mother, and her grandmother behind her other. Her father and brother were outside this framework, while the grandfather was next to the grand-mother.

The woman who sat in the mother's position felt like the central figure and was satisfied with the way she was taking care of everyone. The man sitting in her father's position felt liberated and carefree. The man portraying her brother was facing away from the family and enjoying his life.

Kayoko's grandmother had already died, but the woman who represented her saw her position as one of satisfaction with the life she had made for herself.

Up to this point, the family sculpture represented a family situation that is fairly common in Japan. However, the man who represented Kayoko's grandfather suddenly began trembling and weeping softly. Of course, this man had never met Kayoko's grandfather, and he had died long before Kayoko was born, so she did not know him either, so this was very strange.

"I'm feeling aggrieved," the man said through his tears.

I asked Kayoko how her grandfather had died.

"He was killed in the war," she replied. Then she suddenly added, "I think I know why I feel that I was fated to meet my boyfriend." She continued her story,

"The man I am seeing comes from the same kind of family as I do. That's why I felt that I was fated to meet him. I realize that his mother takes care of everything in the family. Maybe I sensed somehow that he came from the same kind of family, and that overlapped with memories of my own family to create a feeling that I just felt in my bones.

"My grandmother sent my mother an invisible message about a belief that she had developed during those impoverished postwar years: 'Women have no option but to struggle through somehow.' My mother then passed that same message on to me.

"My grandmother also took on the regrets and grievances of my grandfather, who died young in the war. I sense that deep down, she felt aggrieved at being a victim of a war that no one was able to resist.

"She must have knelt in front of his picture on the family's Buddhist altar and held quiet conversations with him: 'If you were alive, you would have found your life's purpose in some kind of work,' or maybe she said, 'If only you were alive, you would have found some hobby to enjoy,' or 'If you were alive now, you could have enjoyed walks in the countryside.'

"That's when she decided to let her son, my father, do the things that her husband couldn't do and to give him the freedom that her husband never had.

"My mother continued that and has always given the men in the family their freedom. I now realize that I did the same with my first husband. I took such good care of him that I was more a mother than a wife."

This case showed me one aspect of transgenerational effects, and that is that the body moves toward love. As Kayoko so aptly put it, the body brings partners to you.

Unconsciously and unaware, we are like those Buddhist statues in that we are always fixing our eyes on something. Sometimes, that "something" may be a distant ancestor. Sometimes, it may be some children we see when we're out and around in the city. Sometimes, it is even a deceased parent. It's not that we stare at them. Without intending to see them, we continue to see them.

5.3 What Transgenerational Effects Tell Us

Case 16: Reunion with a Deceased Mother

Kyoko Fujisawa told me that she'd had the same experience twice in two weeks.

"I've seen my deceased mother. The first time, it was a woman on the train who approached and spoke to me, and I had an intuitive feeling that she was my mother. There were butterflies flying around outside the window of the train at that moment.

I know it's an odd thing to say, but that's what I thought, somehow.

"A week later, I was taking a walk in the countryside when I came upon a small shop that stood all by itself. As I passed by, the owner called to me to stop in and offered me tea. We talked about various things, and I thought, 'My mother is here.' There were butterflies flying around then, too, huge swallowtail butterflies.

"I was not present when my mother died, and I'm haunted by regrets about that. I lived with my mother, and one day, she left the house, saying that she was going out shopping, but she never returned.

"The whole family looked for her, but we couldn't figure out what had happened to her. Three or four days later, the police contact me. My mother had collapsed in a nearby park and been taken to the hospital, they said. She did not have any identification on her, so it took some time for them to find me.

"When I think of my mother dying alone, I think, 'That must have been so hard,' and 'She must have felt so lonely.'

"My father died in a freak accident, and I wasn't with him, either. I wanted to at least take care of my mother, and the thought that I couldn't do that drives me almost crazy with regret. For the longest time, I haven't been able to talk about the fact that my parents died in those ways.

"That's why I felt that my mother came to me during those two weeks. I don't know why I felt that way, but I was sure that it was true."

This is what Kyoko told me, weeping as she spoke. And wouldn't you know it, as she was speaking, a flock of butterflies passed by the window.

A System for Conveying Love

Our eyes are always moving, just like the eyes of an eagle. They never stop. If they do stop, we become unable to see things and shapes.

At the same time I began to study Gestalt therapy, I also started to study the Feldenkrais Method, which seeks to develop the neurons in the brain through physical movements. This is what my teacher, Carl Ginsburg, told me: "If I fix myself so that nothing moves and the image stays on the retina for so many seconds, I will no longer see."

We don't see all the shapes, colors, and sizes that are reflected onto our eyes. We distinguish and choose what we want to see. If I see something from the window of my room—let's assume that it is a book—I assign a meaning to the thing that I saw, discover it, distinguish it, and perceive it to be a book.

Ginsburg also said, "My perception is organized to see a particular thing."

Thinking in these terms, it may be fair to say that Kyoko Fujisawa saw her mother when she was emotionally prepared to do so.

It may also be true that Kayoko Yokomine's "family pattern" rose from subconscious to conscious awareness when she wanted to see the connection between her beliefs about fate and her family.

Transgenerational effects are not necessarily negative legacies. The families that produce us are systems for conveying love to the next generation. Normally, we recall memories of our families as quietly and impassively as stone Buddhas, but at times, we have to look closely at the unfinished business created by our families.

*   *   *

One morning, instead of waking up as soon as the sun seeped into my room as I usually do, I dozed off on my futon for several minutes. I lazily rolled over. At that moment, my left eye opened slightly, and I saw a murmuring stream filled with crystal-clear water.

The scene made me believe that a little girl could talk to plants. I caught a glimpse of the world in which my little daughter could hold conversations with pill bugs. Then, like a bubble bursting, the scene disappeared, and, somewhat to my regret, I was back in the real world.

Afterword

This book asks the question, "What are transgenerational effects?" At the same time, it also asks what a family is. For twenty-five years, I have been steadily learning about Gestalt therapy, a psychological therapy that asks about the individual's responsibility for situations. Of late, I have become aware of how much of my life I have spent on this pursuit.

Gestalt therapy is not well known in Japan, but in the West, all therapists and counselors learn the basics of it. In many countries, it has been incorporated into the medical system and is covered by insurance, so that is one reason for its widespread use.

In Japan, however, few people can teach Gestalt therapy, and no systems for learning it have been established, so it is not in wide use. That is why I founded the Japan Association of Gestalt Therapy (JAGT) in January 2010. It now has about 250 members and ten branches, including some in every region of the country. I anticipate that JAGT will continue to grow little by little.

The reason that I began writing about transgenerational effects was that I wanted people to learn about one aspect of Gestalt therapy.

Gestalt therapy focuses on the individual's life, so, inevitably, concerns about the family that formed the background of the individual's life should emerge. That is because I have noticed that relations between the individual's patterns of life and his or her family of origin are a major issue for many people. The motivating energy behind writing this book was to make people aware that there is a mutually supportive system that lies behind most tensions and conflicts within a family.

Awareness is important not only for the purposes of therapy and healing but also rather for sparking creativity. In fact, many Gestalt therapists overseas are active in professions not directly connected with psychology, such as the arts or philosophy, an indication of just how wide-ranging this form of therapy is.

I wish individuals would incorporate awareness into their lives so that they would be full of energy and able to live a fulfilling life and daily routine.

People are born into and grow up in families. Almost as a matter of course, love is transmitted to the next generation, which receives it and passes it on to the generation after that. This chain is the essence of transgenerational effects.

We are mammals who are oriented toward living in groups, members of a phylum that acquired emotions through evolution in order to protect the groups, or families, that they belong to. The source of these emotions is the system for creating the strong ties among family members that we refer to as "love."

But what happens when these ties of love are incomplete? If they remain as unsolved problems among the members of the family, a negative transgenerational effect arises. In order to cast some light on what happens, I have cited actual case studies, although of course, I have changed the clients' names.

Buddhism teaches the concept of karma, which has become familiar to people around the world. In response to a person's acts in his or her lifetime, luck (or karmic backlash) is generated. This record of deeds is not lost at death but is transmitted to the person's children and grandchildren, at least according to one of the philosophical theories about destiny known as "karmic luck."

In addition, Japanese culture includes an important custom of revering one's ancestors so that people set up commemorative tablets, observe the O-Bon festival, and mark the anniversaries of family members' deaths by visiting their graves. These customs are deeply rooted in Japanese culture, and they are part of the wisdom of Eastern culture about how to deal with negative transgenerational effects.

I do not use words such as karma, fate, ancestors, or previous lives when discussing negative transgenerational effects, and I have thought about what kind of theories would arise from taking a long look at these issues from the point of view of psychological therapy. The term I have come up with is "transgenerational effects." I think that this expression will give rise to new worldviews that are not looked into in existing traditions.

Words and expressions change over the years, but the essential nature of families does not. Just as they always have, families will continue transmitting love to the next generation.

June 2012

About the Author

Born in 1945 in Niigata, Japan, Masatsugu Momotake graduated from the Chuo University Faculty of Science and Engineering in 1979. He then earned a degree from the Graduate Department of Psychology at California State University (Fresno).

After returning to Japan, he worked at Kanagawa Prefectural Preventative Medicine Association, where he taught yoga and health education that incorporated psychology for breast cancer patients. Over the many years that followed, he worked throughout Japan to introduce Gestalt therapy. In 2010, he founded the Japan Association of Gestalt Therapy (JAGT), having obtained the cooperation of Ansel Woldt, Gordon Wheeler, and Morgan Goodlander in 2009. He served as the association's first president for six years.

He is currently president of the Gestalt Network Japan. He is internationally certified in the Feldenkrais Method. He has conducted workshops in Greece, Canada, the U.S., and Australia. His book *The Gestalt Path of the Mini Satori* has appeared in English.

References

General References

Akira, Ikemi. *Kokoro no Message wo kiku* [Listening to the Messages of the Mind], Kodan-sha Gendai Shinsho, 1995.

Akira, Ikemi. *Boku no* Focusing = Counselling [My Focusing = Counselling], Sogen-sha, 2010.

Mitsuhiro, Denda. *Daisan no nô: Hifu kara kannagaeru inochi, kokoro, sekai* [The Third Brain: Life, Mind, and World Thought from Skin], Asahi Shuppan-sha: 2007.

Akihiko, Takashima. *Omoshiroihodo yokuwakaru nô noshikumi* [Interesting Things about the Brain's Mechanisms], Nihon Bungei-sha: 2006.

Sandra Blakeslee, Matthew Blakeslee. *Nô no nakano shintai-chizu: Body map no okagede, taitei no kotoga umaku iku wake* [The Body Has a Mind of Its Own: How Body Maps in Your Brain Help You Do (Almost) Everything Better]. Translated by Junko, Komatsu, Intershift: 2009.

Kosuke, Oki. *Nô ga kokomade wakatte kita: Bunshi-seirigaku ni yoru "kokoro no kaibô."* [Things We Know about the Brain so Far: "Dissection of Mind" Through Molecular Phygiology], Kobun-sha, 1989.

Motohiro, Yoritomi (Ed.). *Buddha wo shiritai* [Wanting to Know about Buddha], Gakken Publishing, 2011.

Katsunari, Nishihara. *Naizo ga umidasu kokoro* [Mind Created by Organs], NHK Books, 2002.

Takahisa, Tokunaga, (Ed.). *Dondon mega yokunaru magical eye* [Fast Recovery of Sight with Magical Eye], Takarajima-sha, 2004.

Moshé Feldenkrais. *Nô no meiro no bôken: Feldenkrais no chiryo no jissai* [The Case of Nora: Body-Awareness as Healing Therapy], translated by Takeshi Yasui, Sojin-sha, 1991.

Carl Ginsburg. "Body-Image, Movement and Consciousness." Published in its final form in the *Journal of Consciousness Studies*, 6, No. 2: 3, 1999, pp. 79-91.

Reference Related to Family and Group Relationship
Vimala, Inoue. *Jinsei de taisetsuna itsutsuno shigoto: Spiritual care to bukkyo no mirai.* [Five Important Tasks in Life: Spiritual Care and the Future of Buddhism], Shunjyu-sha, 2006.

E. Kübler-Ross. *Shinu shunkan* [On Death and Dying], translated by Sho, Suzuki, CHuko-bunko, 2001.

Bert Hellinger; *Datsu-Psychotherapy-ron* [Acknowledging what is: Conversation with Bert Hellinger], translated by Kiyo Nishizawa, Mediart Publishing Corporation, 2009.

Bert Hellinger. Ai no hôsoku: shitashii kankei deno kuzuna to kinkô [Love's Own Truth], translated by Mami, Kobayashi, Osho Enterprise Japan, 2007.

Ken Wilber. Integral Spirituality, translated by Taro Matsunaga. Shunjyu-sha, 2008.

Akira, Aoki; Takashi, Kubo; Retsu, Koda; Norio, Suzuki; Introduction to Integral Theory Volume 1 | Ken Wilber's Unified Theory of Human Consciousness, Shunjyu-sha, 2010.

John Bradshaw. *Family secret kuzutsuita tamashii no tameno kazokugaku* [Family Secret: What You Don't Know *Can* Hurt You], Translated by Yasuko, Kasaki, Aoyama Publishing, 1995.

Gestalt Therapy-Related Literature
Japanese Association of Gestalt Therapy. *Gestalt Ryoho Kenkyu* [Gestalt Therapy Study], Vol. 1, 2011.

Takashi, Kubo. *Somachikku shinrigaku* [Somatic psychology], Shunjyu-sha, 2011.

F. S. Perls. *Gestalt ryoho: sono riron to jissai* [The Gestalt Approach and Eye Witness to Therapy], supervised and translated by Yoshiya Kurato, Nakanishiya Shuppan, 1990.

Masatsugu, Momotake. *Empty chair technique nyumon.* [An Introduction to the Empty Chair Technique], Kawashima Shoten, 2004.

Masatsugu, Momotake. *Kizuki no therapy: Hajimete no gestalt ryoho* [Therapy of Awareness: An Introduction to Gestalt Therapy], Shunjyu-sha, 2009.

Perls, F. S., Hefferline, R. F., and Goodman, Paul. *Gestalt therapy.* Calif. The Real People Press, 1969.

Bo Lozoff, *We're all doing time*; Hanuman Foundation, 1985.

Abraham H. Maslow, *Maslow on Management*; John Wiley & Sons, 1998.

Ansel L. Woldt, Sarah M. Toman, *Gestalt Therapy*; Sage Publication, 2005.

James I. Kepner; Body Process; *A Gestalt Institute of Cleveland Publication*, 1987.

www.ingramcontent.com/pod-product-compliance
Lightning Source LLC
Chambersburg PA
CBHW071337290326
41933CB00039B/1174